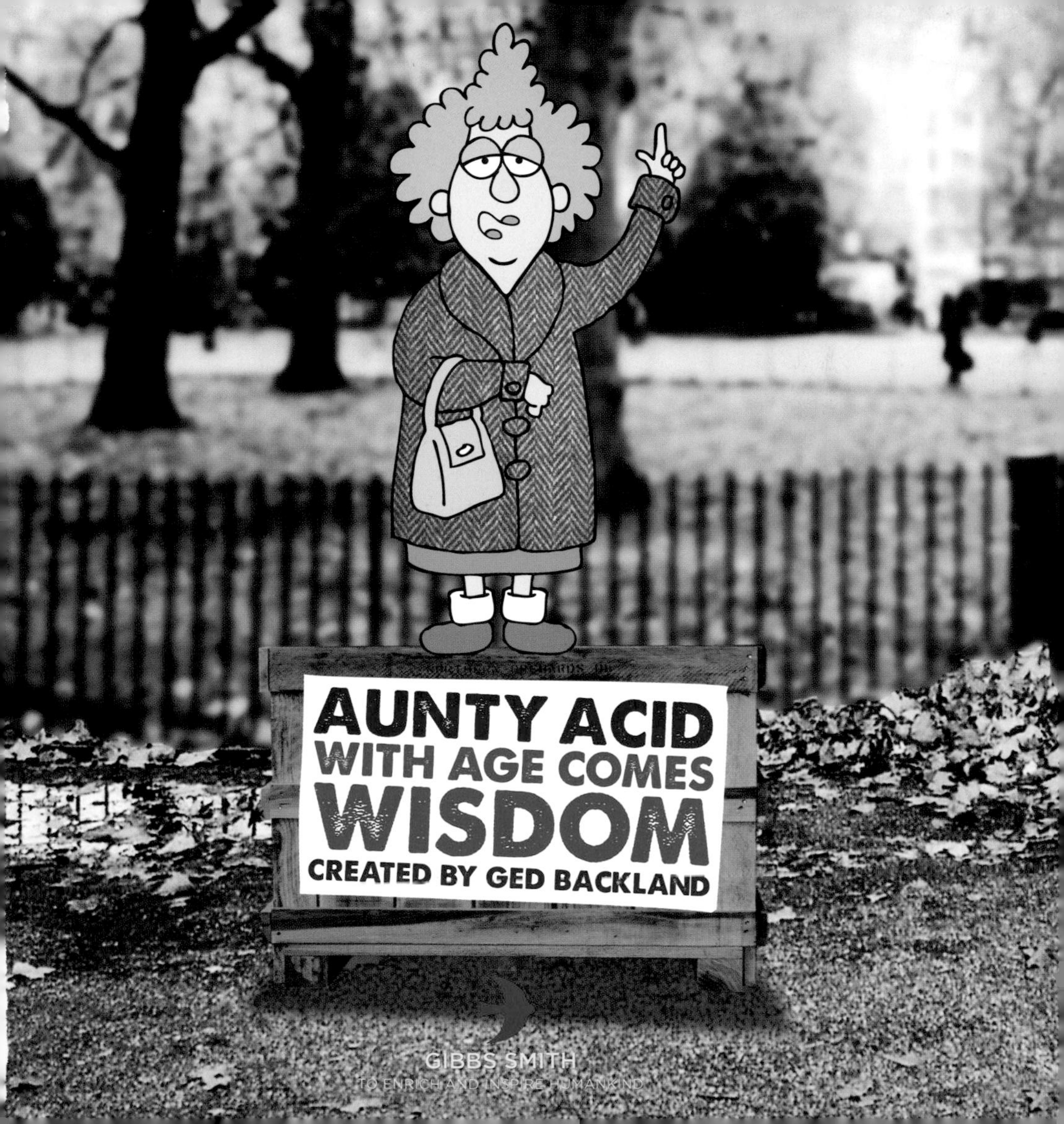
AUNTY ACID
WITH AGE COMES
WISDOM
CREATED BY GED BACKLAND

GIBBS SMITH
TO ENRICH AND INSPIRE HUMANKIND

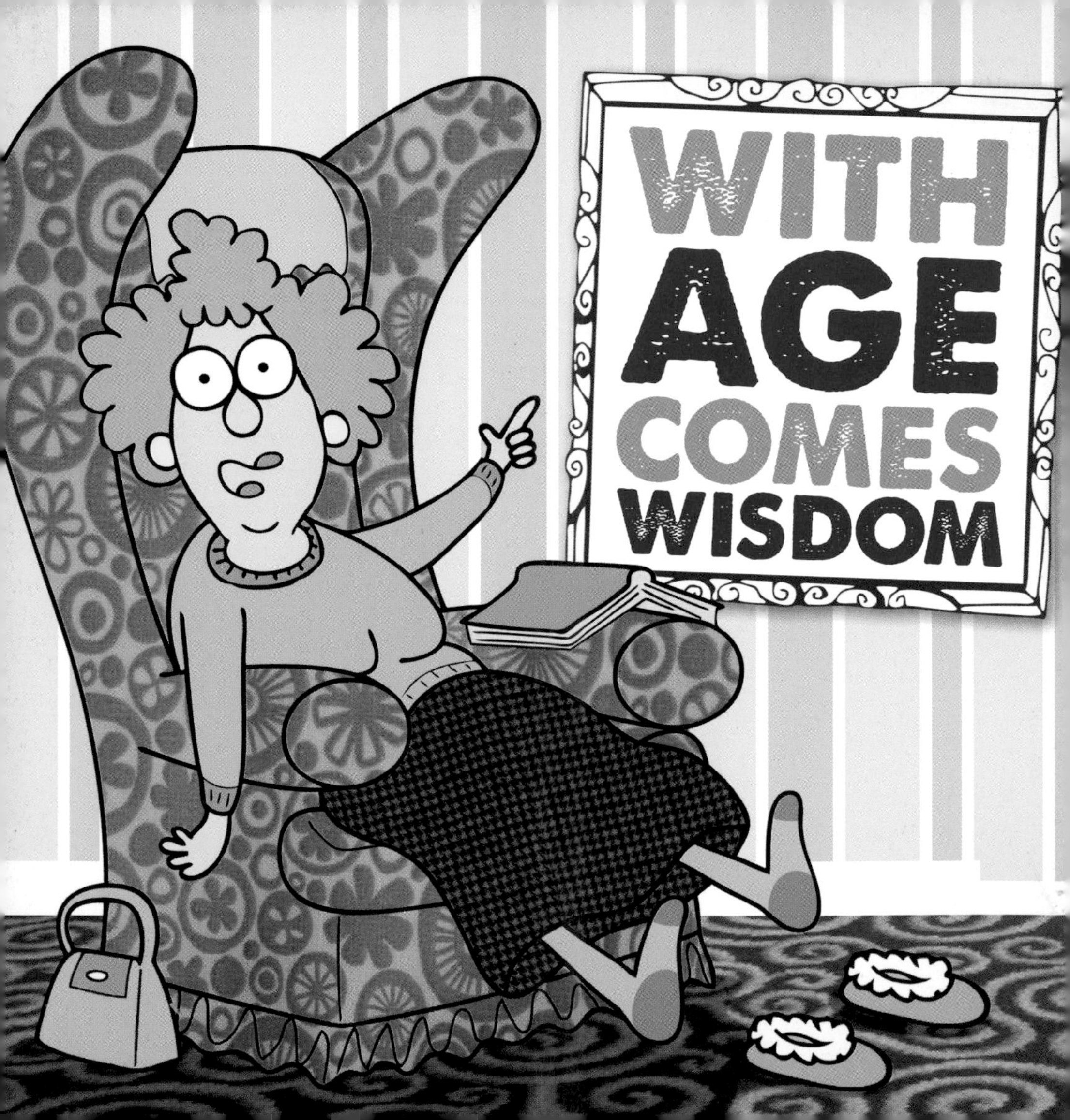
WITH AGE COMES WISDOM

BUT SOMETIMES AGE COMES ALONE...

I've been on this planet a freakin' long time and no, before you ask, I'm not telling you how long. A gal's gotta keep a few secrets to herself!

I'll just say my first job after college was as a waitress at the Last Supper. In fact, I'm so old that now I'm starting to poop dust!

Well you know what? In all my years, I've collected a whole bunch of wisdom along the way—like the best way to get a man to do something is to tell him he's too old for it. If we really **DO** learn from our mistakes, I've made so many that I ought to be a freakin' genius!

There's a whole bunch of my wisdom here in this little book and, hopefully, it will help you take the roller coaster of life with a pinch of salt, a slice of lemon (from those that life keeps handing you) and a slug of tequila.

WISE WORDS ON
DIET & EXERCISE

Let's face it, gym bunnies make us all look bad.

I mean look at them, they're done. "Nice job stick insect, now go home."

It's really people like us who need to be here. These days, I manage just about five sit-ups ever morning—I can only hit the snooze button that many times before it overrides my laziness.

It's all about self-love. I'm not FAT, I'm just so freakin' sexy it overflows.

Hope all the laughter you'll get from this section helps burn off those troublesome calories. It's got my wise words on everything from how to burn 3,000 calories in 20 minutes (leave the pizza in the oven too long) to calling your toilet "the gym," so you can tell everyone you go to the gym first thing in the morning, every single day.

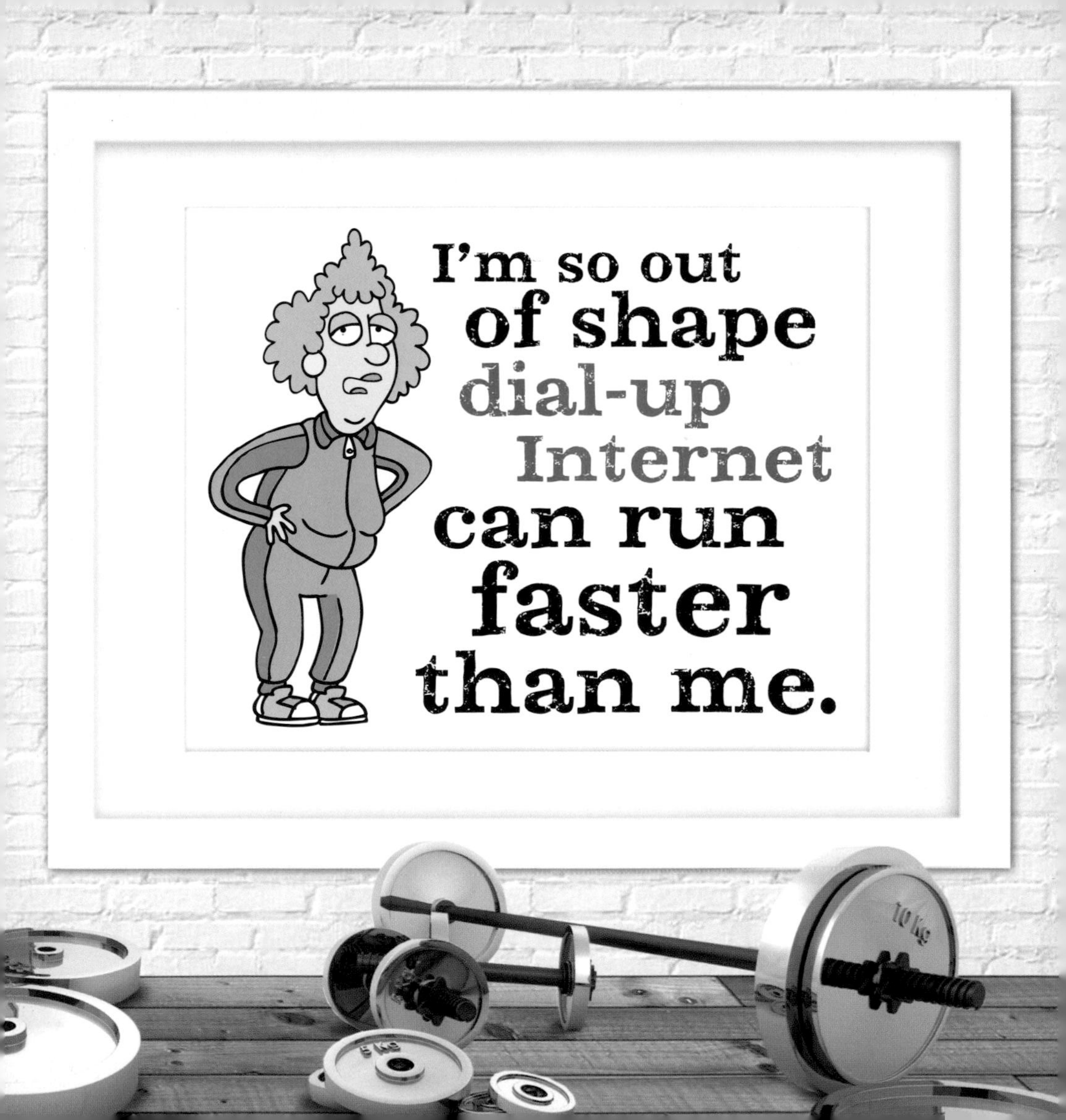
I'm so out
of shape
dial-up
Internet
can run
faster
than me.
10 kg
5 kg

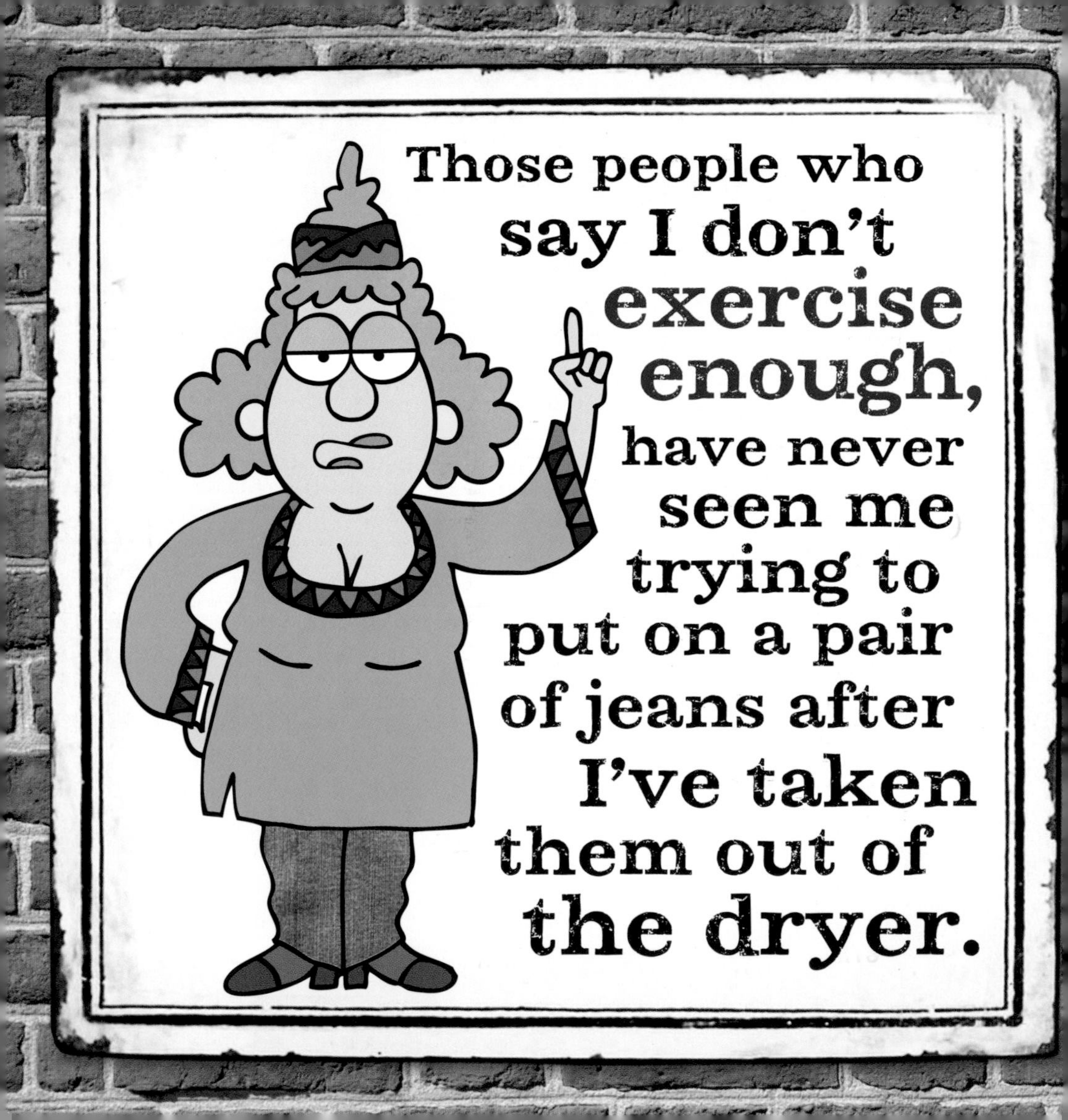
Those people who say I don't exercise enough, have never seen me trying to put on a pair of jeans after I've taken them out of the dryer.

My favorite exercise at the gym is lateral neck turns. I walk in, shake my head, think, “No way!” and walk out again.

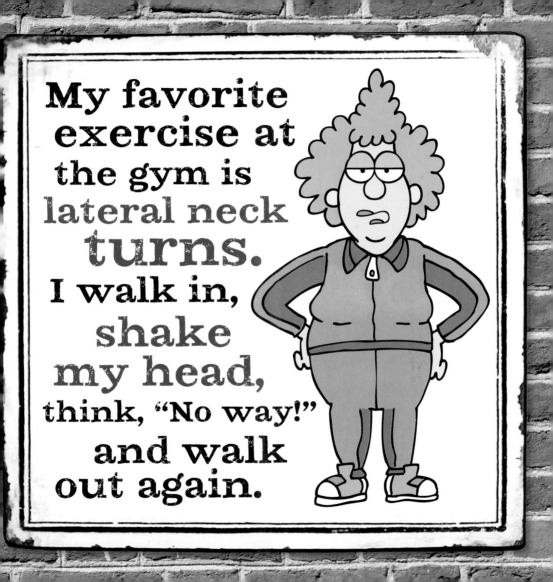

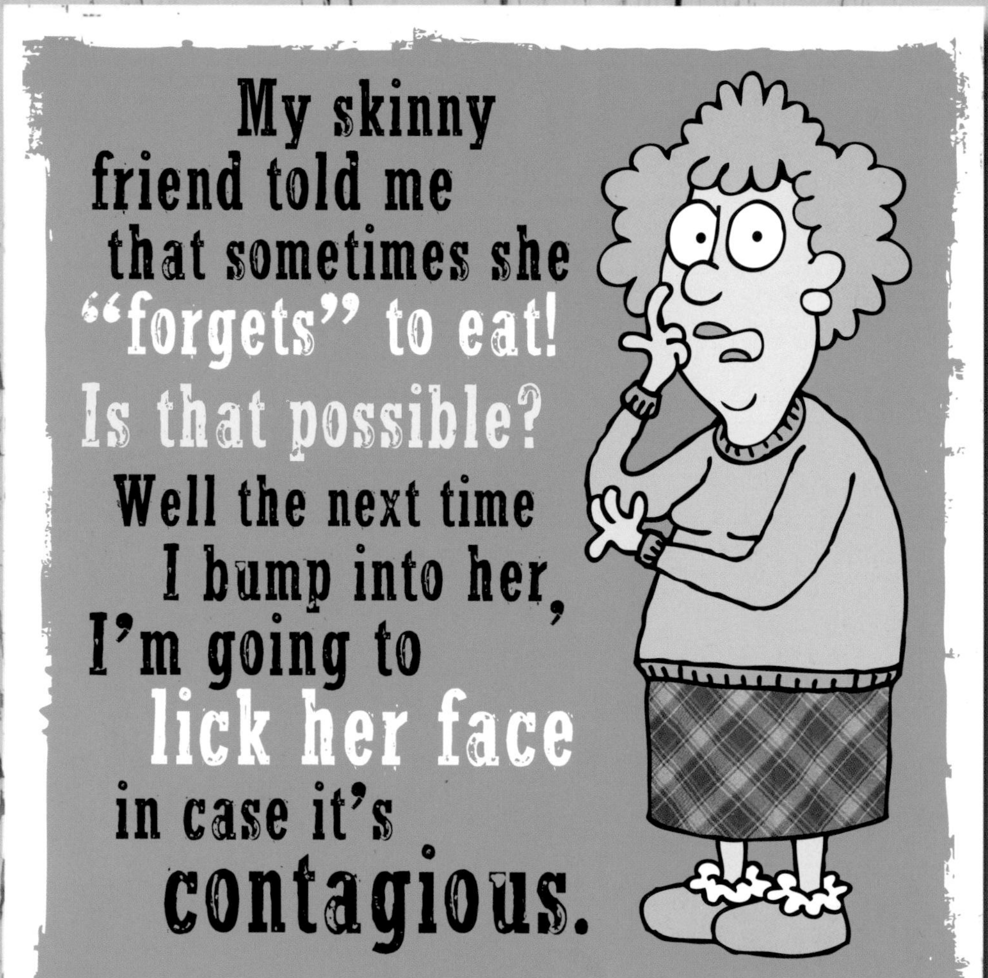
My skinny
friend told me
that sometimes she
"forgets" to eat!
Is that possible?
Well the next time
I bump into her,
I'm going to
lick her face
in case it's
contagious.

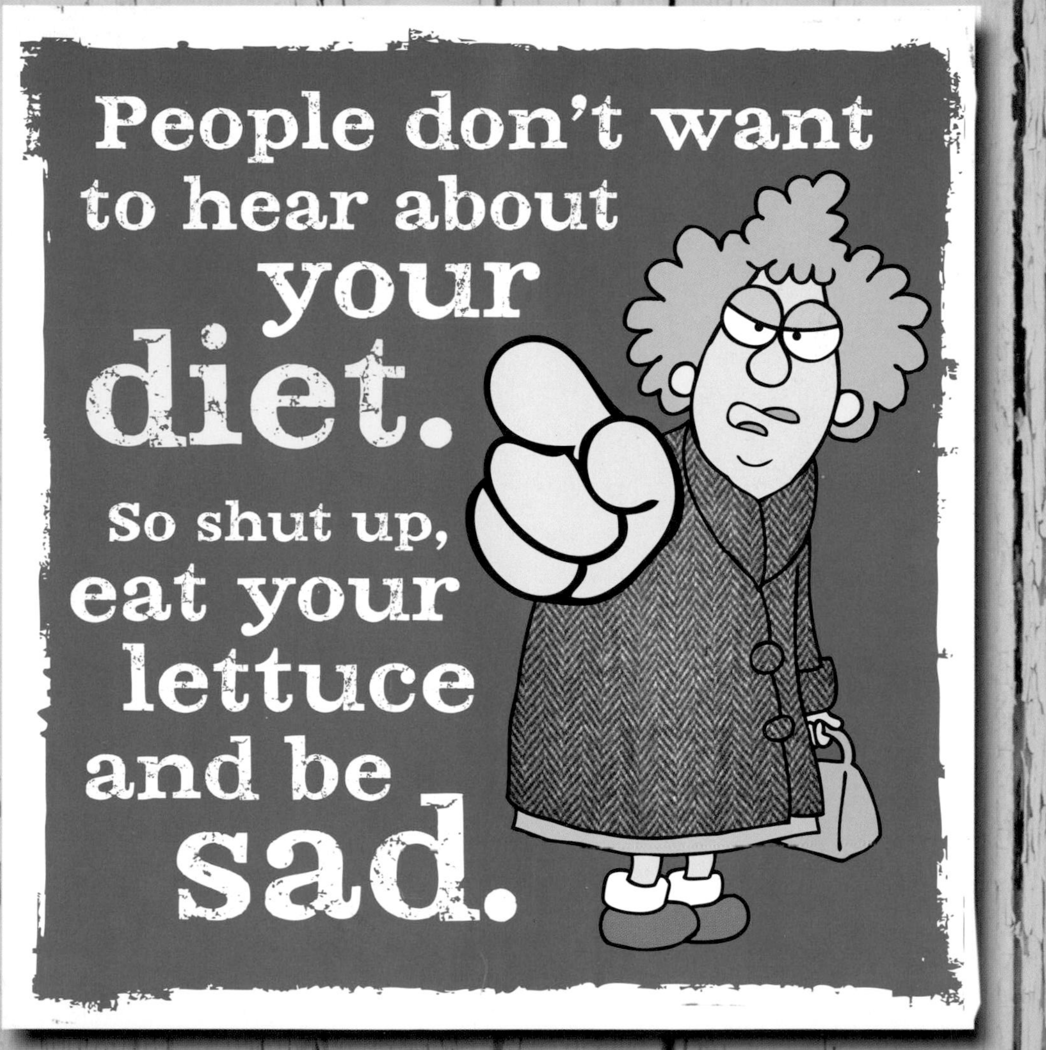
People don't want to hear about your diet.
So shut up, eat your lettuce and be sad.

Being on a treadmill for an hour is really good.

Next week I think I'll start walking.

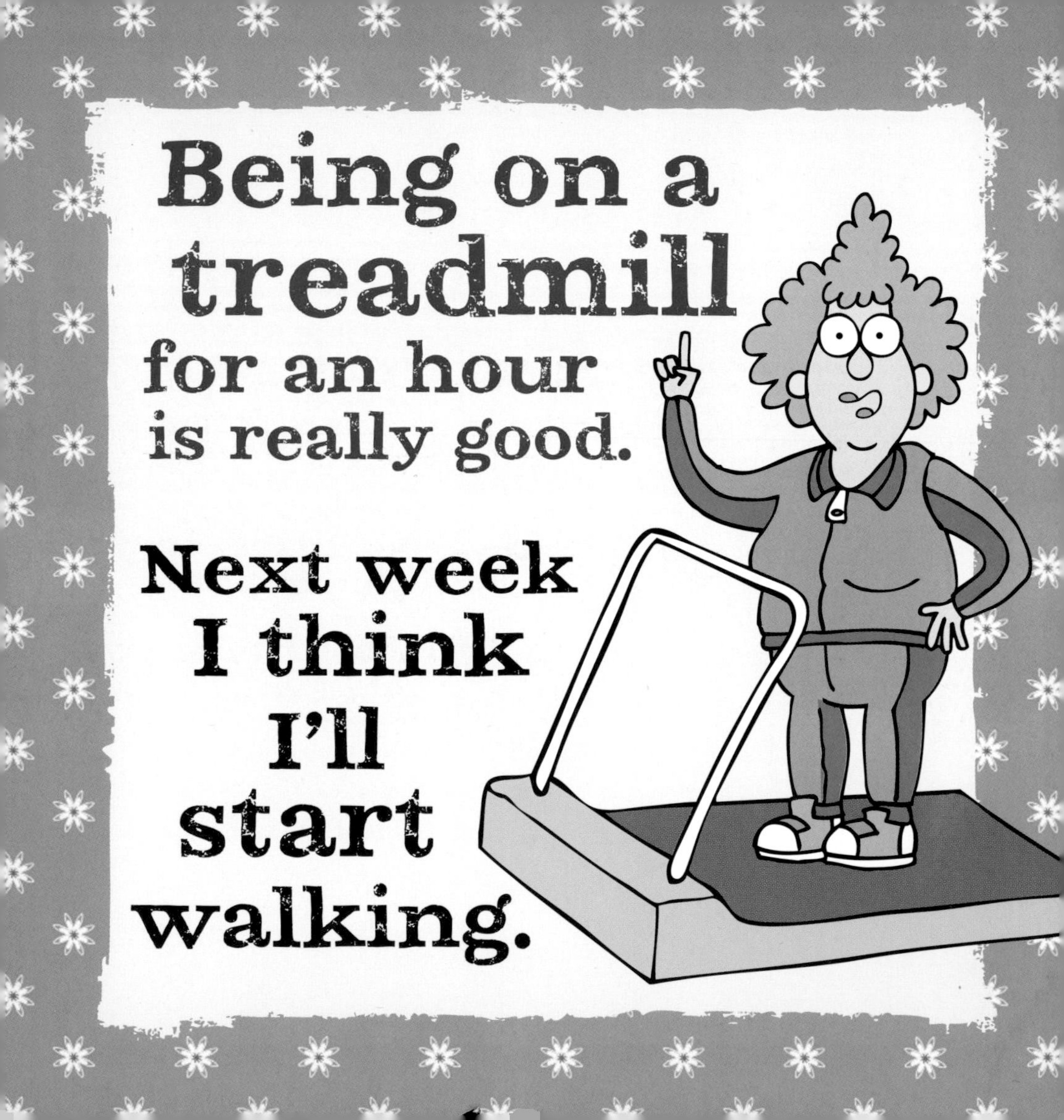

YOGA...

If you haven't
farted
yet,
you're
not doing
it right.

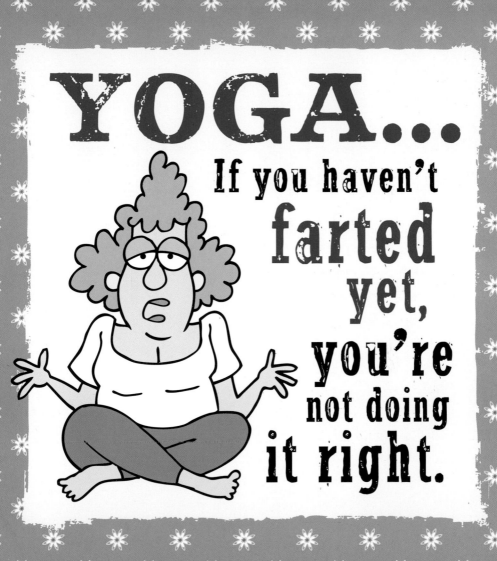

Sometimes I wish

I was a cat

...because

the fatter

you are

the more people

like you.

Plus you get

to sleep

all day.

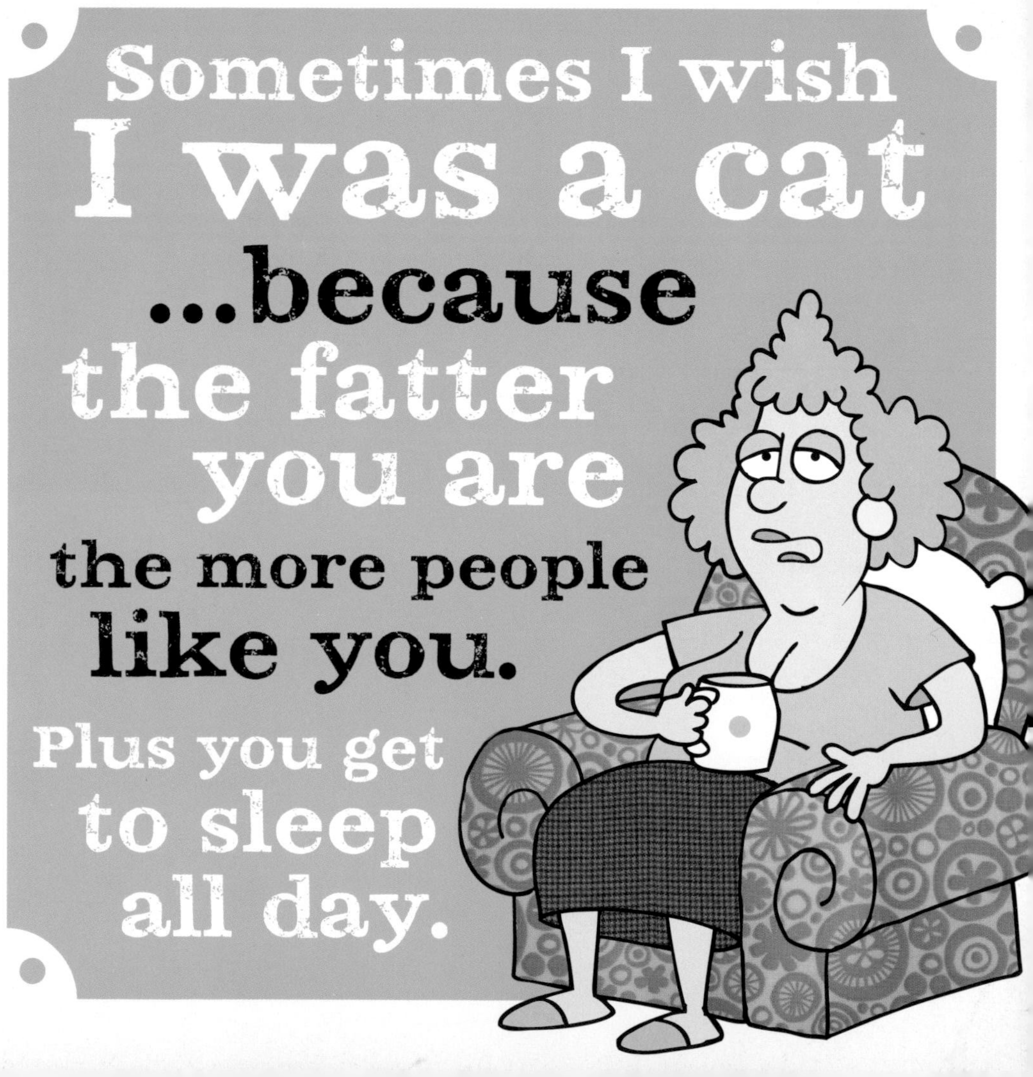

I just ran five miles **and what a workout!** I didn't think that **ice cream truck** would ever stop.

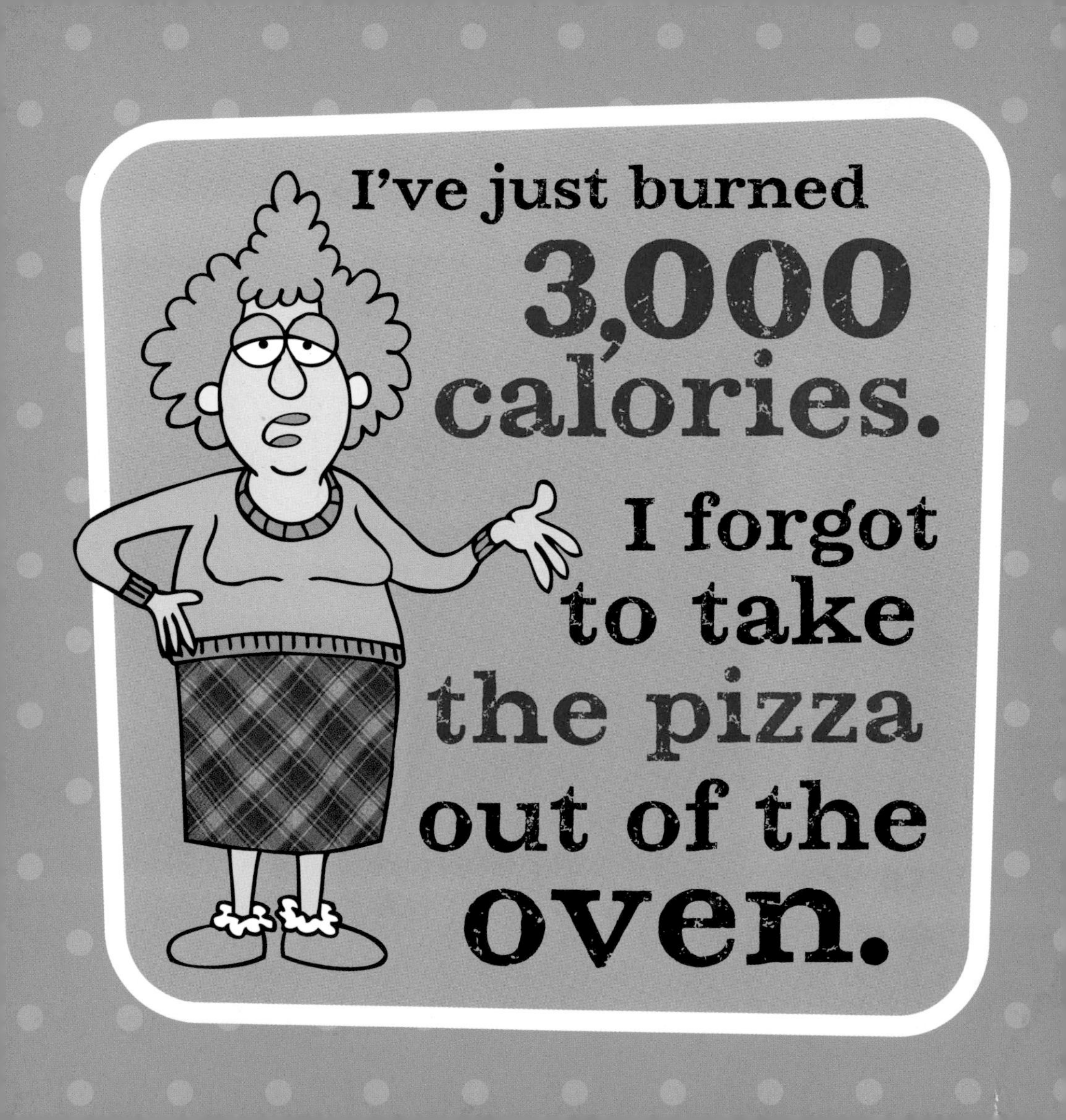

I've just burned 3,000 calories. I forgot to take the pizza out of the oven.

My body is
a temple
...but
nowadays
my steeples
point the
wrong way.

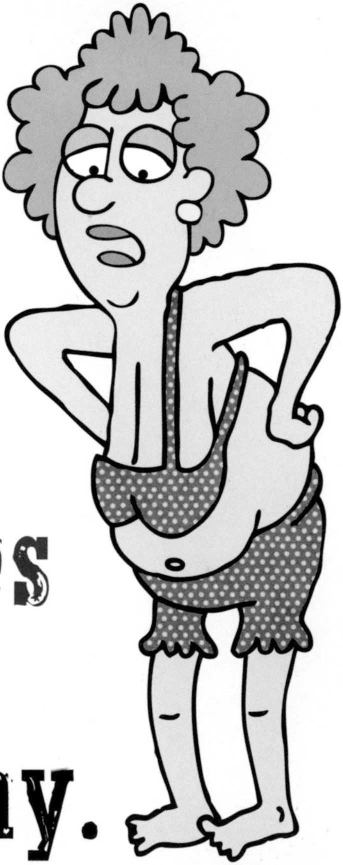

HEY, GYM BUNNIES!

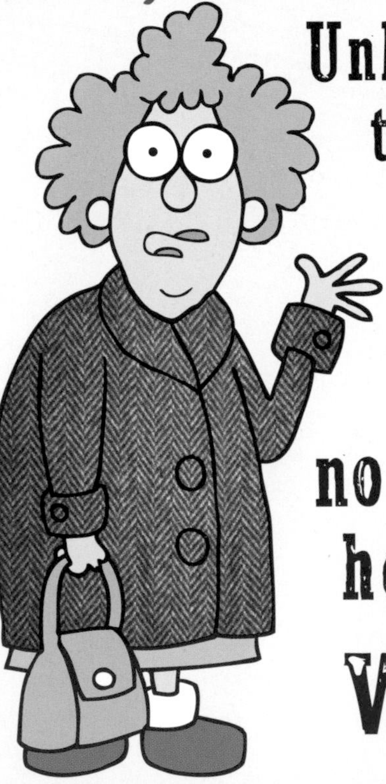

Unless you fell off the treadmill and **smacked your face,** no one wants to hear about your **workout.**

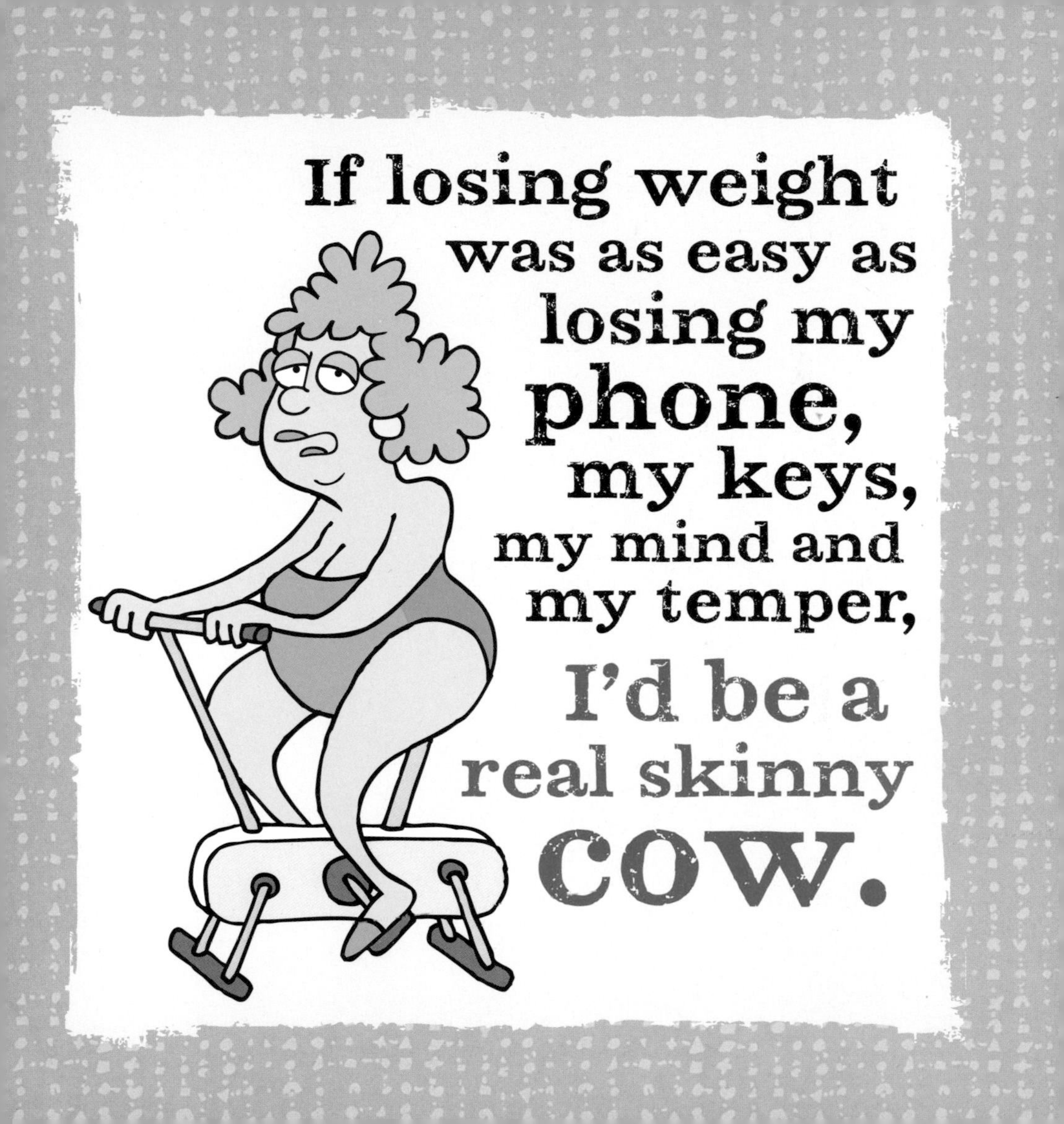

If losing weight
was as easy as
losing my
phone,
my keys,
my mind and
my temper,
I'd be a
real skinny
cow.

AUNTY ACID'S
HEALTH CHECK
NO.27

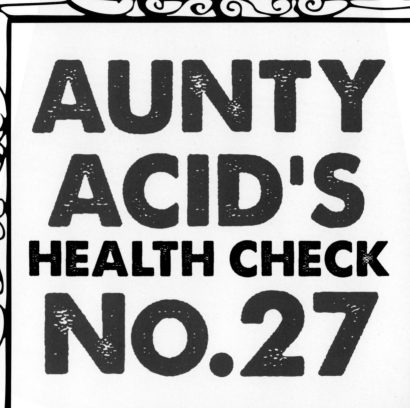

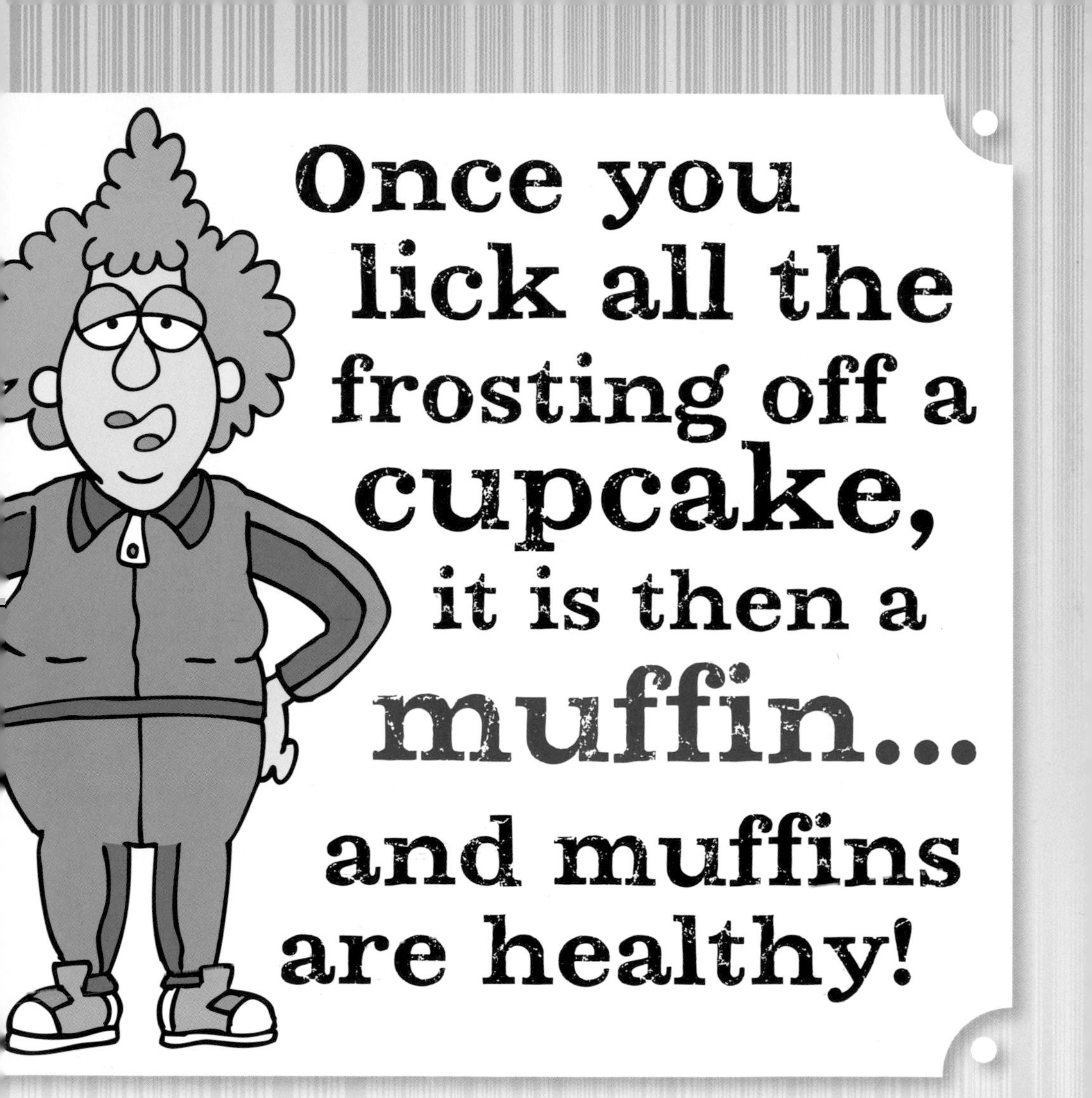

Once you
lick all the
frosting off a
cupcake,
it is then a
muffin...
and muffins
are healthy!

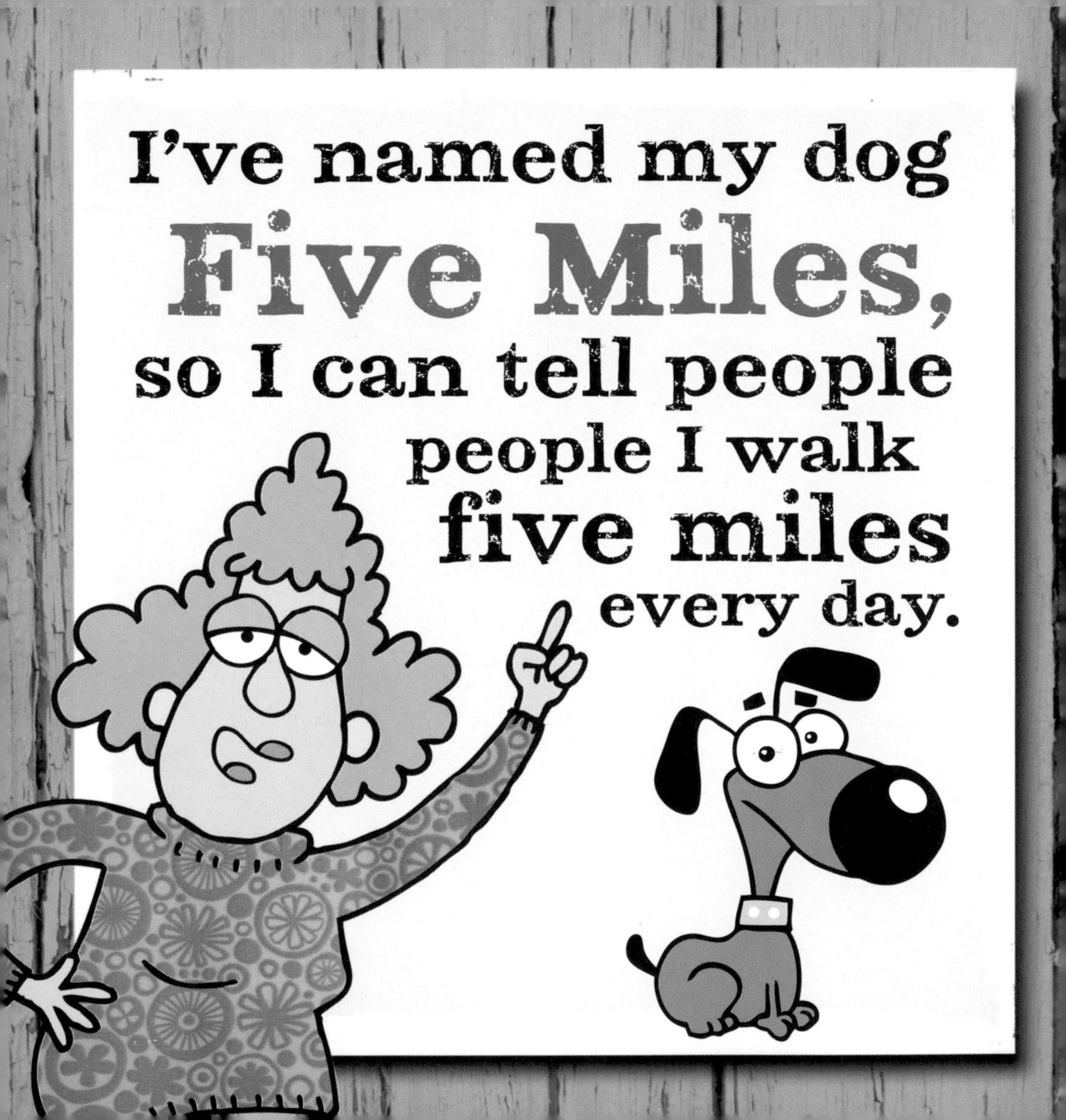
I've named my dog
Five Miles,
so I can tell people
people I walk
five miles
every day.

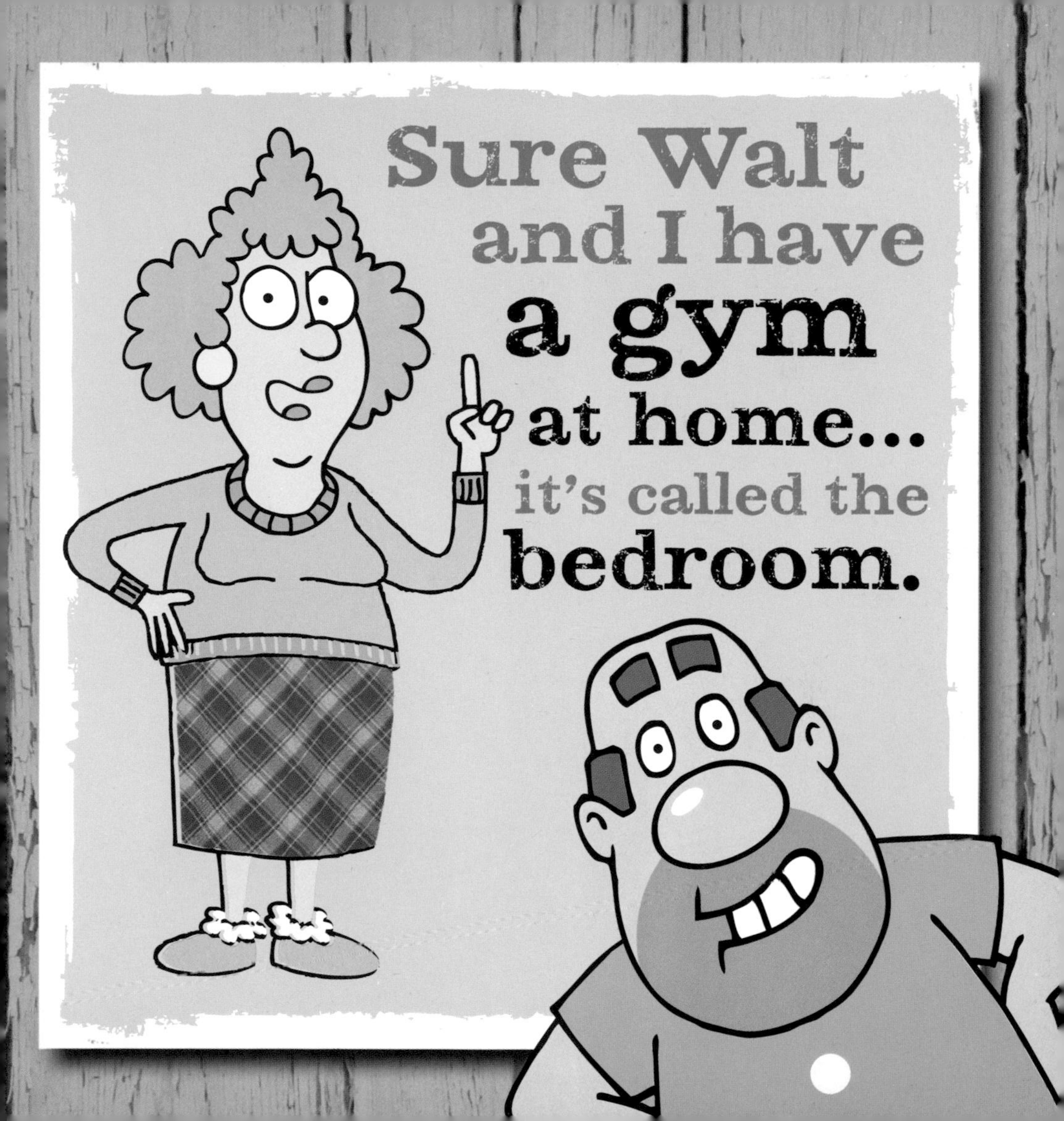
Sure Walt
and I have
a gym
at home...
it's called the
bedroom.

WISE WORDS ON LIQUOR

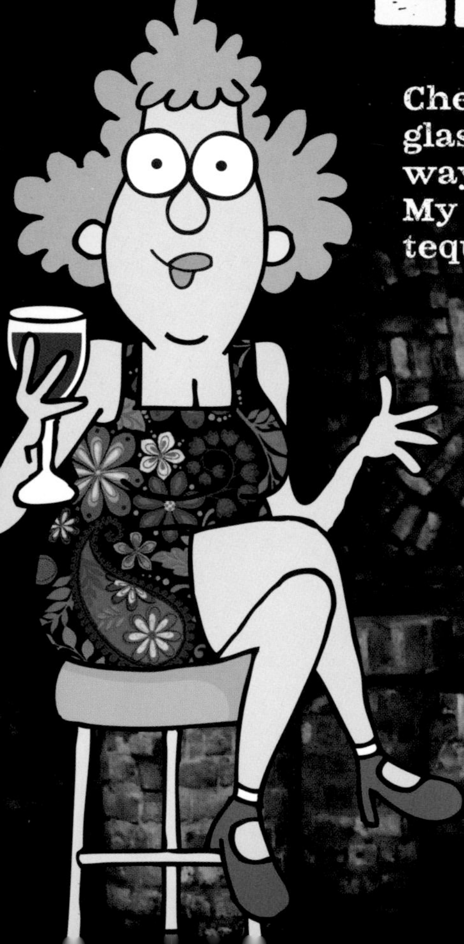

Cheers! I've always enjoyed a fine glass of wine, after all it is the way us classy people get loaded. My motto is one tequila, two tequilas, three tequilas—floor!

I have alcohol to thank for some of the best times I'll never remember. Here's a fact just for all those who think alcohol is a problem, it turns out it's a solution. Thanks, science!

In alcohol's defense, I've done some pretty dumb stuff when I've been sober, too.

Carry on reading all my sassy sayings on everything from shots to beers and whiskey to wine.

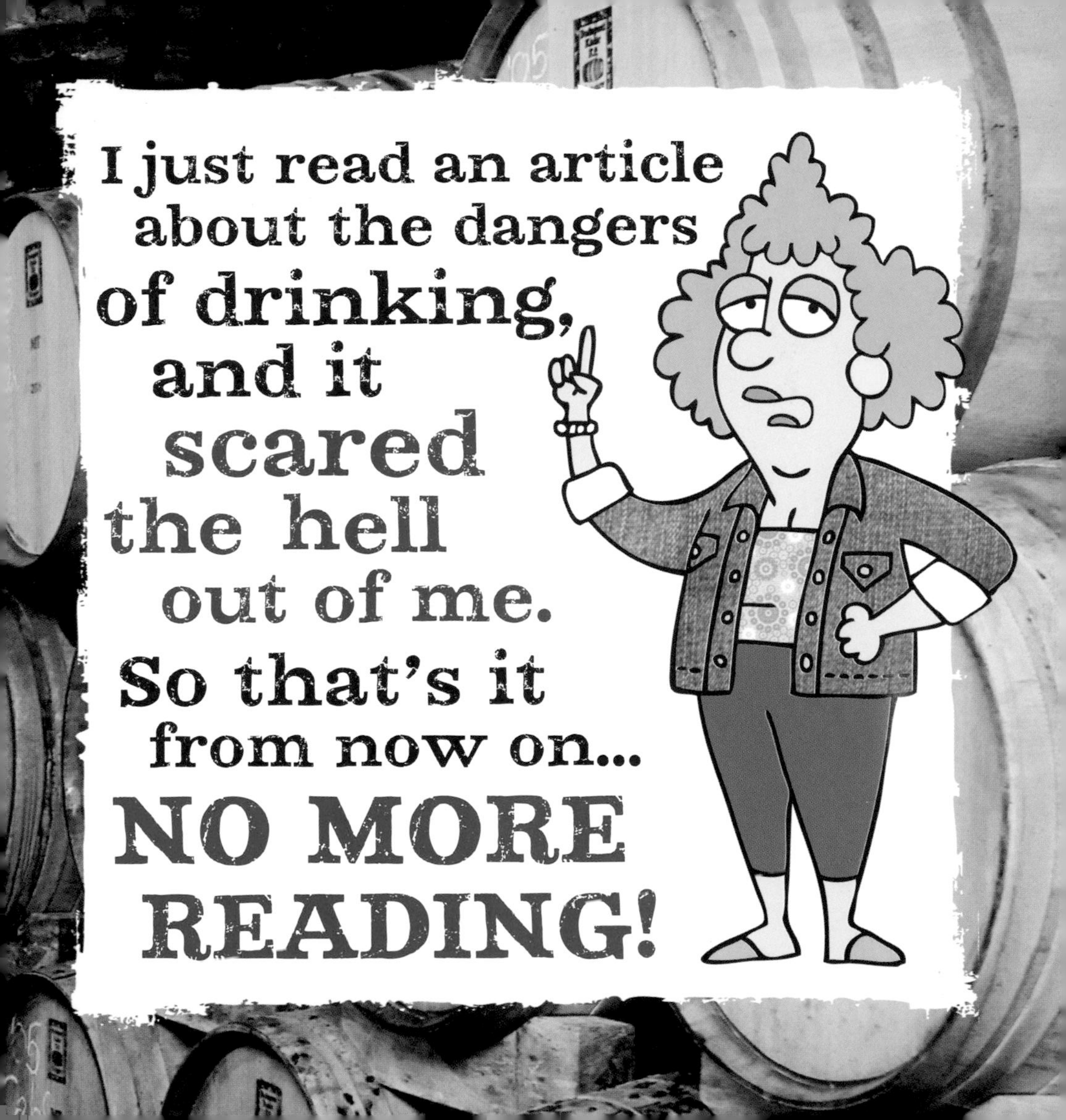
I just read an article about the dangers of drinking, and it scared the hell out of me.
So that's it from now on...
NO MORE READING!

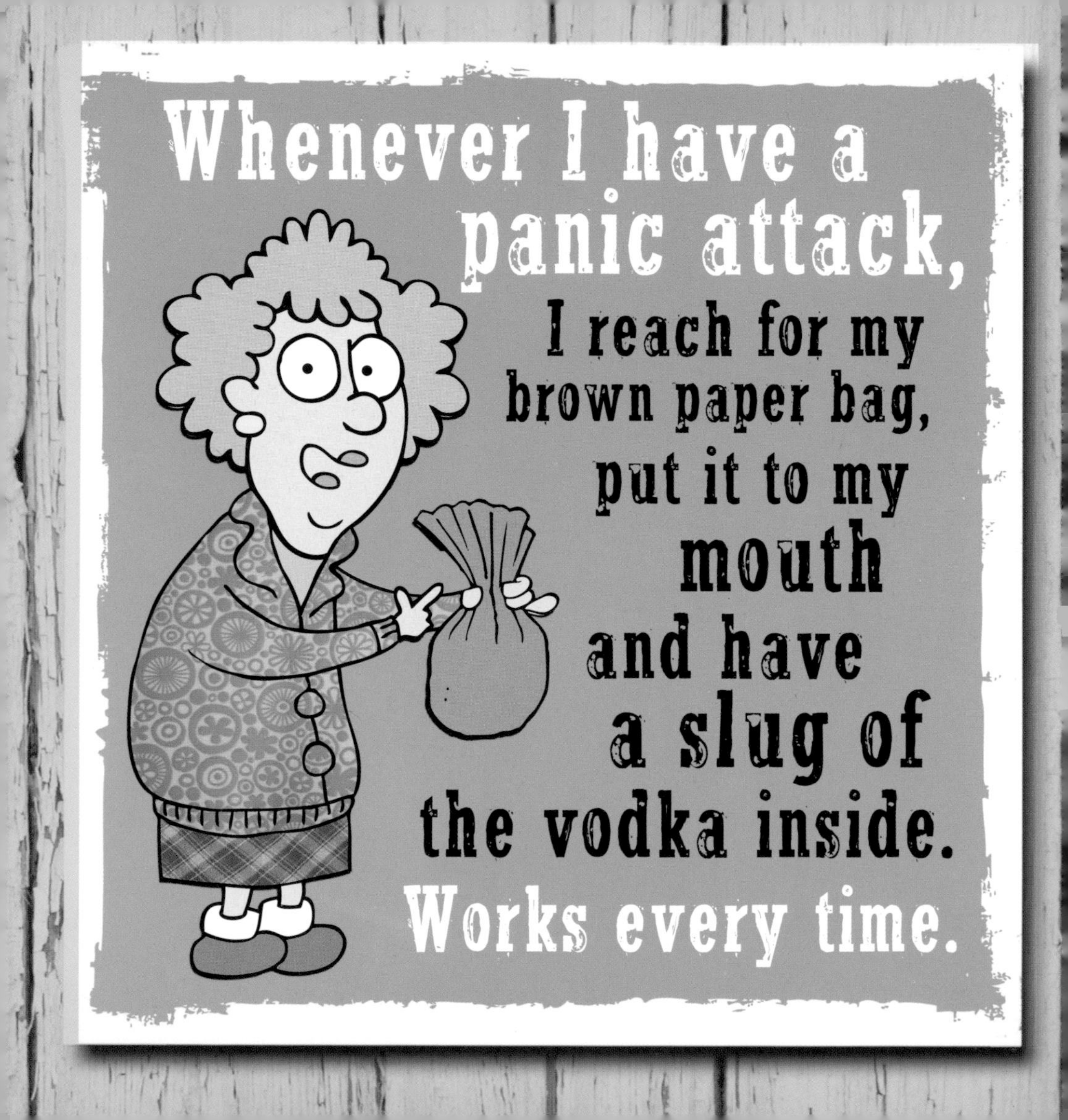
Whenever I have a panic attack,
I reach for my brown paper bag, put it to my mouth and have a slug of the vodka inside.
Works every time.

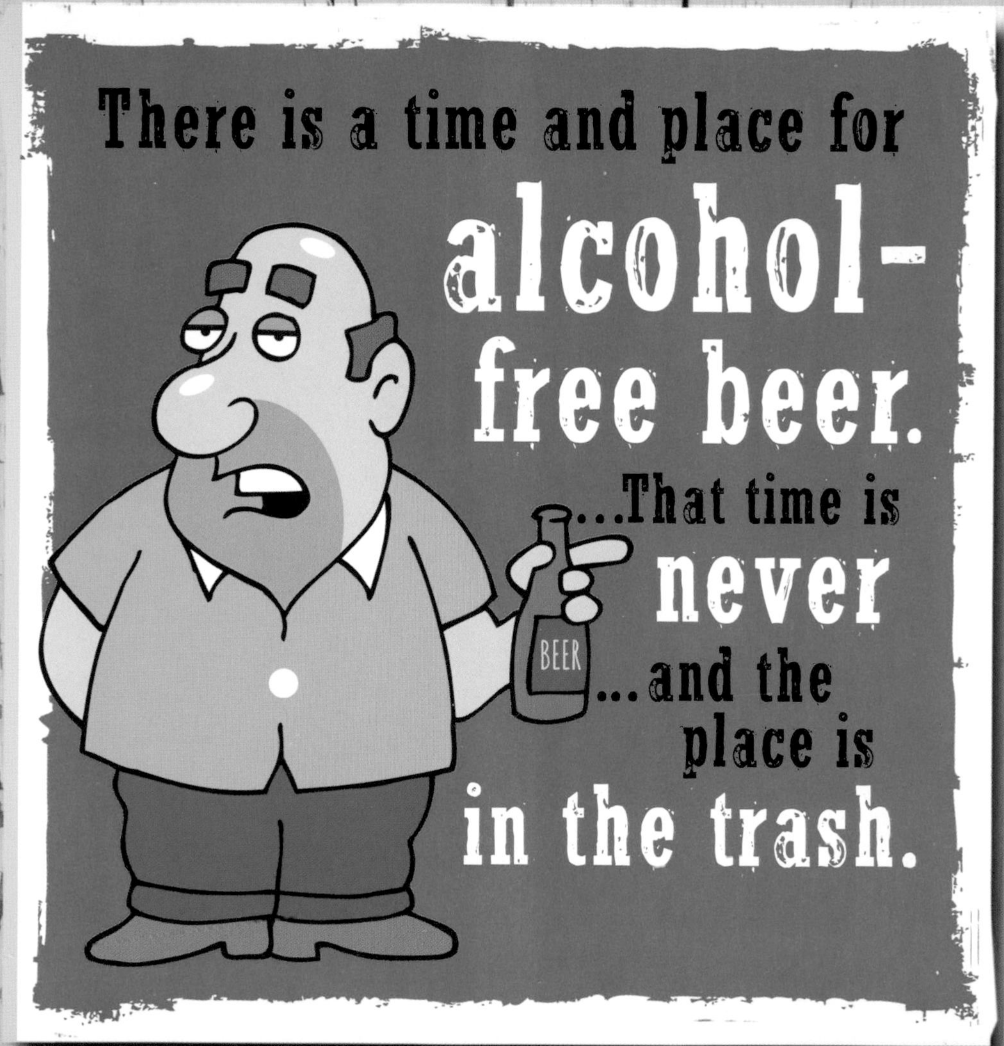
There is a time and place for
alcohol-
free beer.
...That time is
never
...and the
place is
in the trash.
BEER

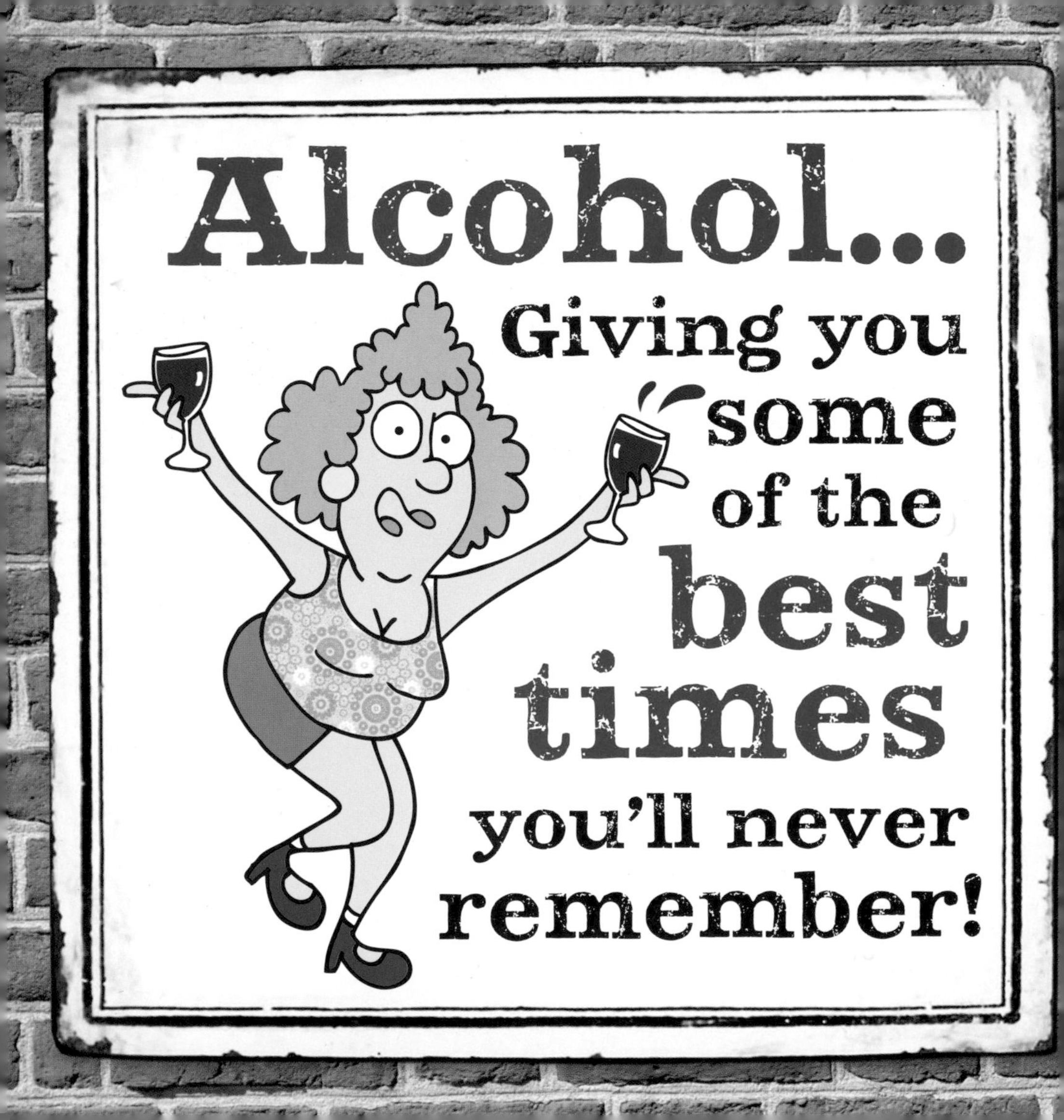
Alcohol...
Giving you some of the best times you'll never remember!

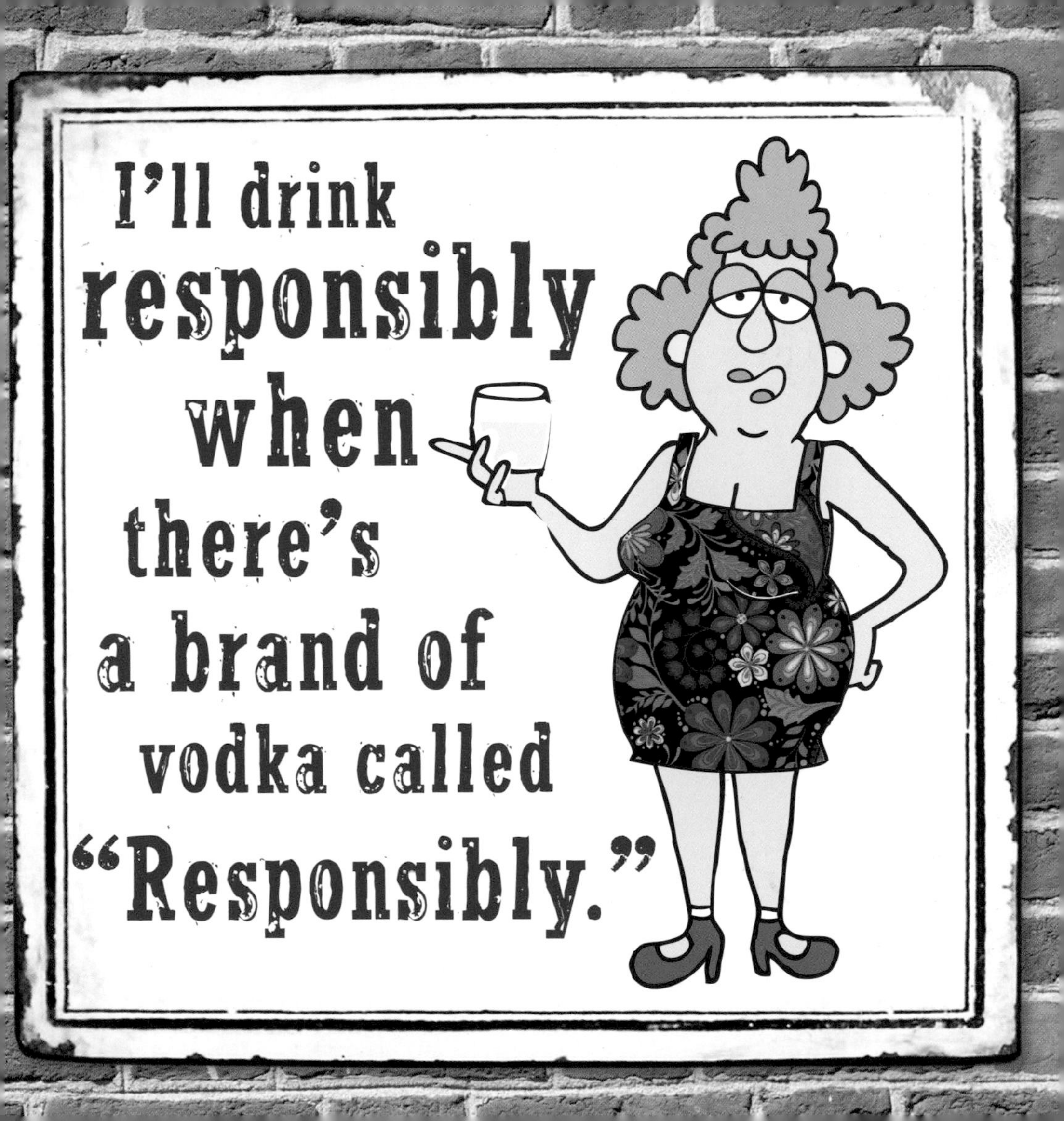
I'll drink
responsibly
when
there's
a brand of
vodka called
"Responsibly."

WALT'S DRINKING RULE NO.1

It's not considered **drinking alone** if the dog is home.

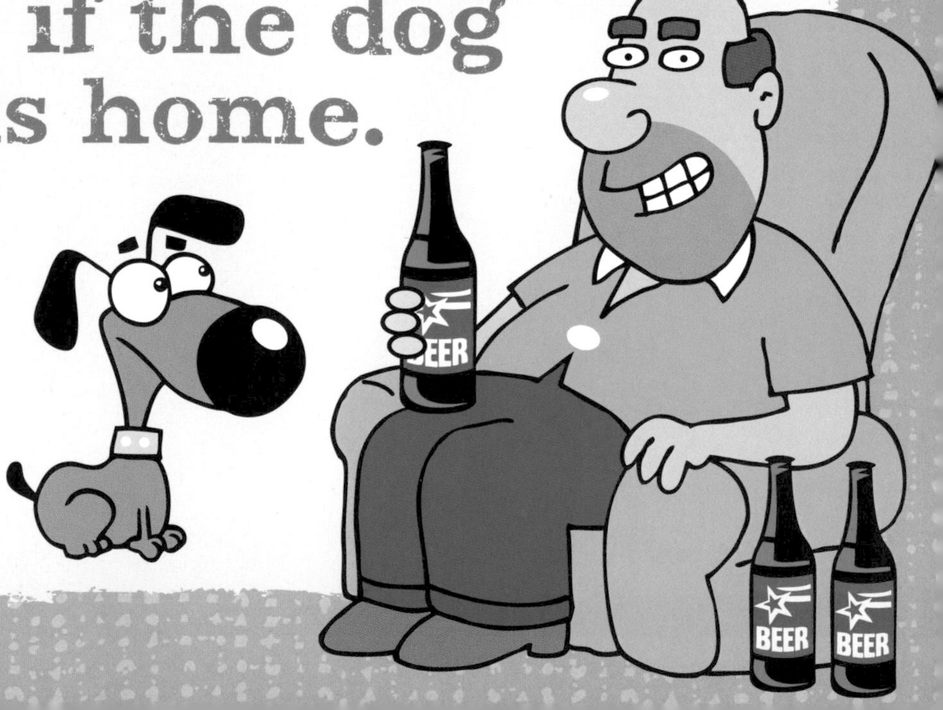

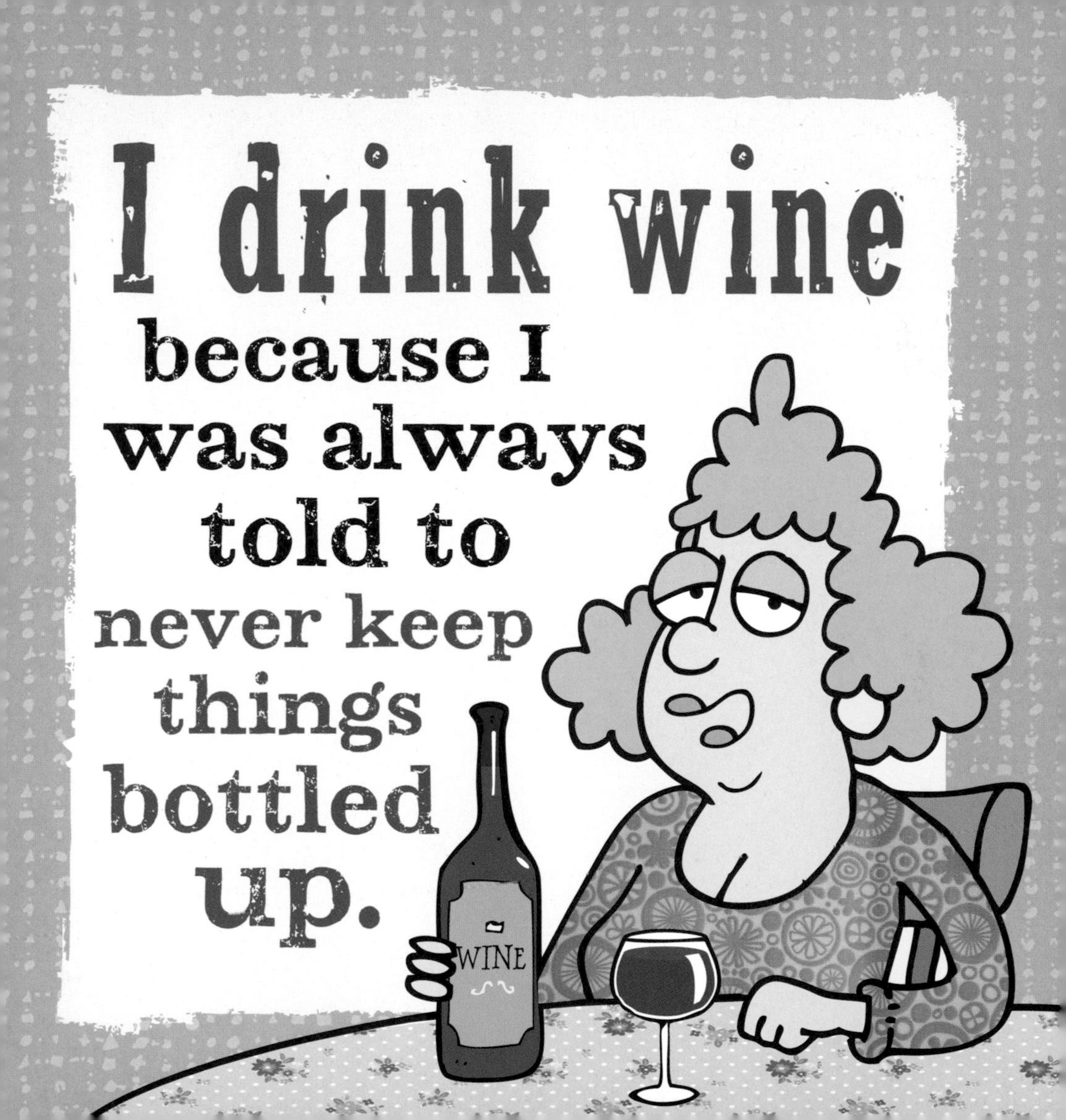
I drink wine
because I
was always
told to
never keep
things
bottled
up.
WINE

Tequila helps me appreciate the small things in life

...like shot glasses.

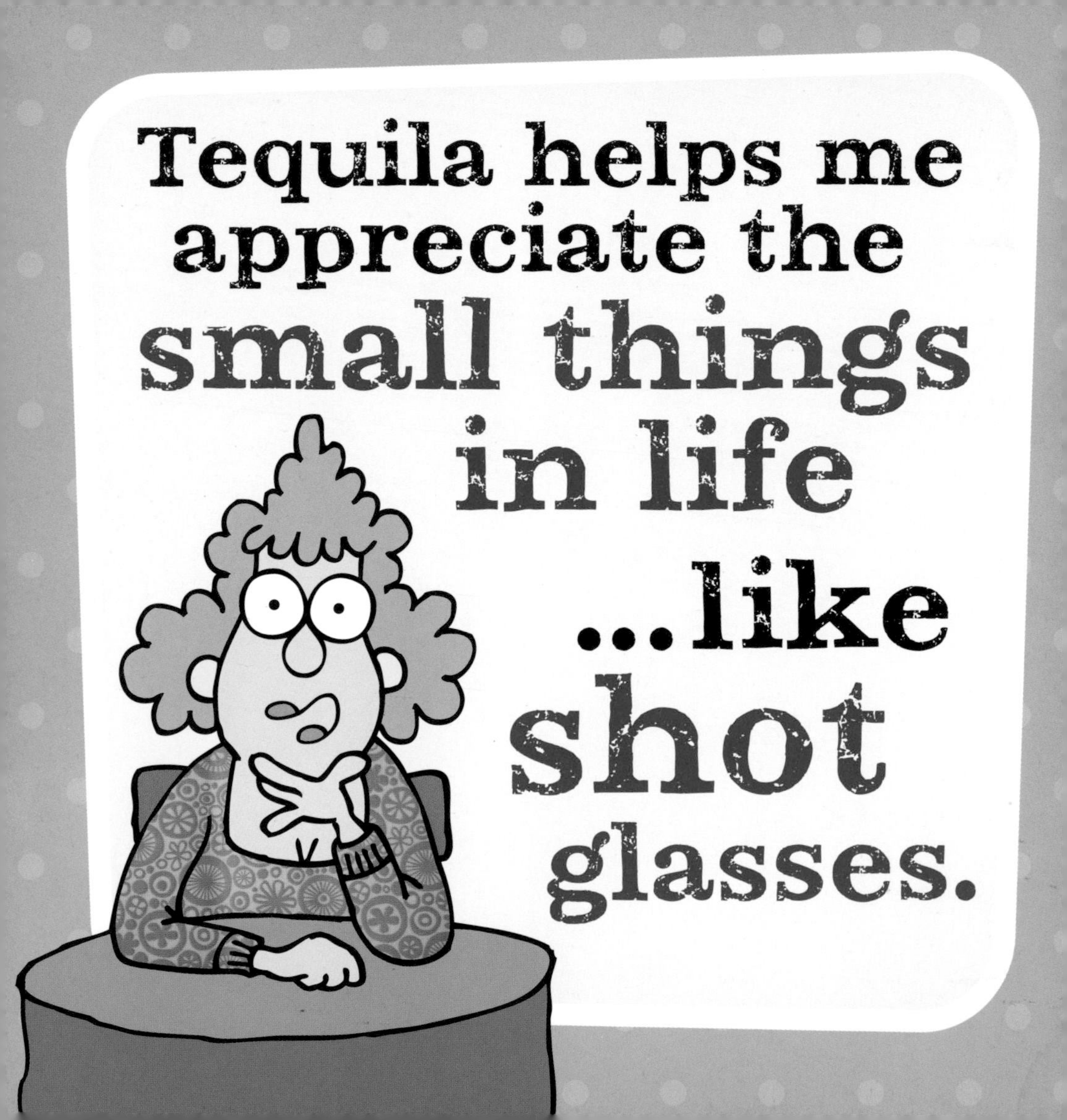

Drunk is when you feel sophisticated

...and can’t pronounce it.

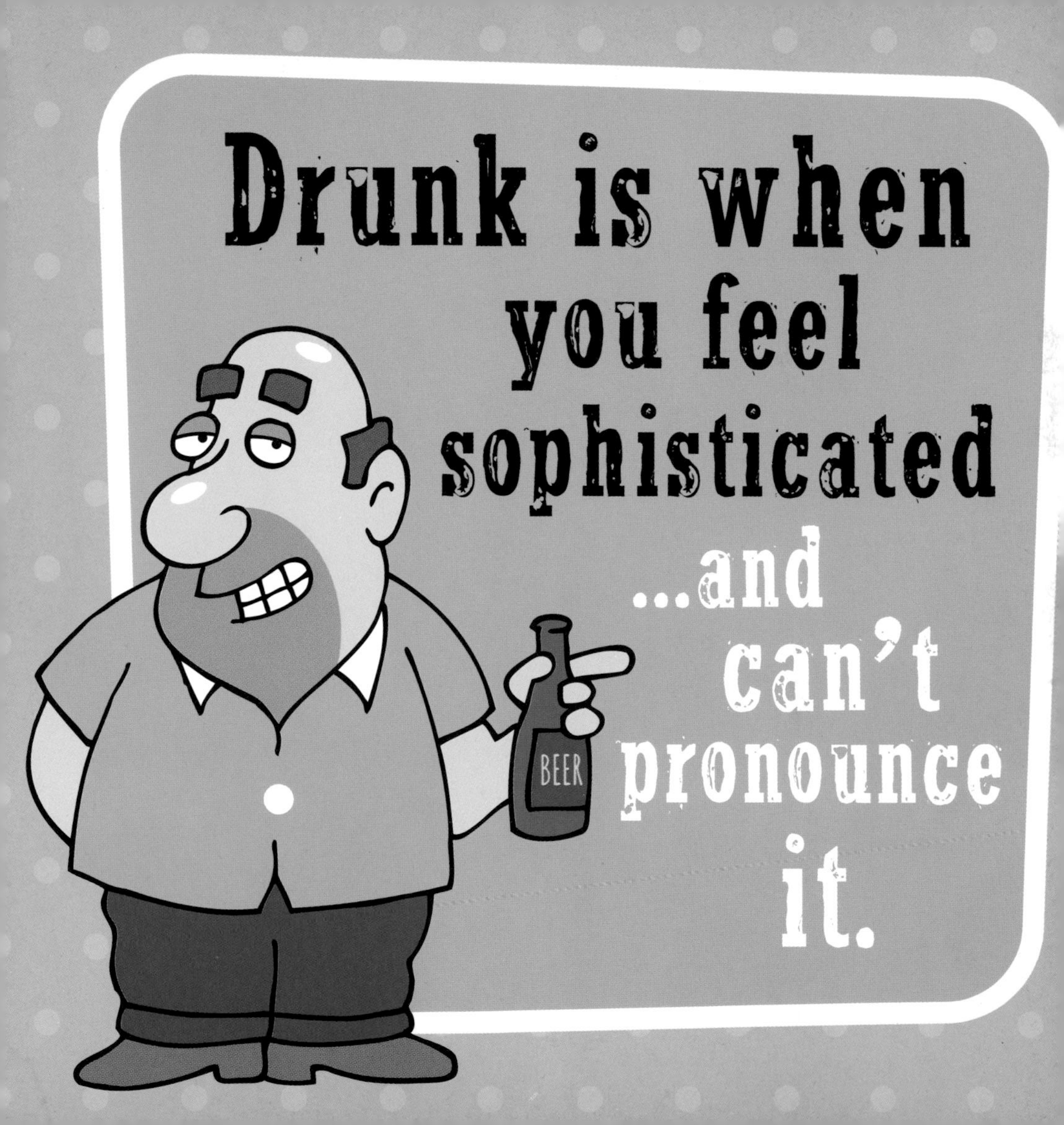
BEER

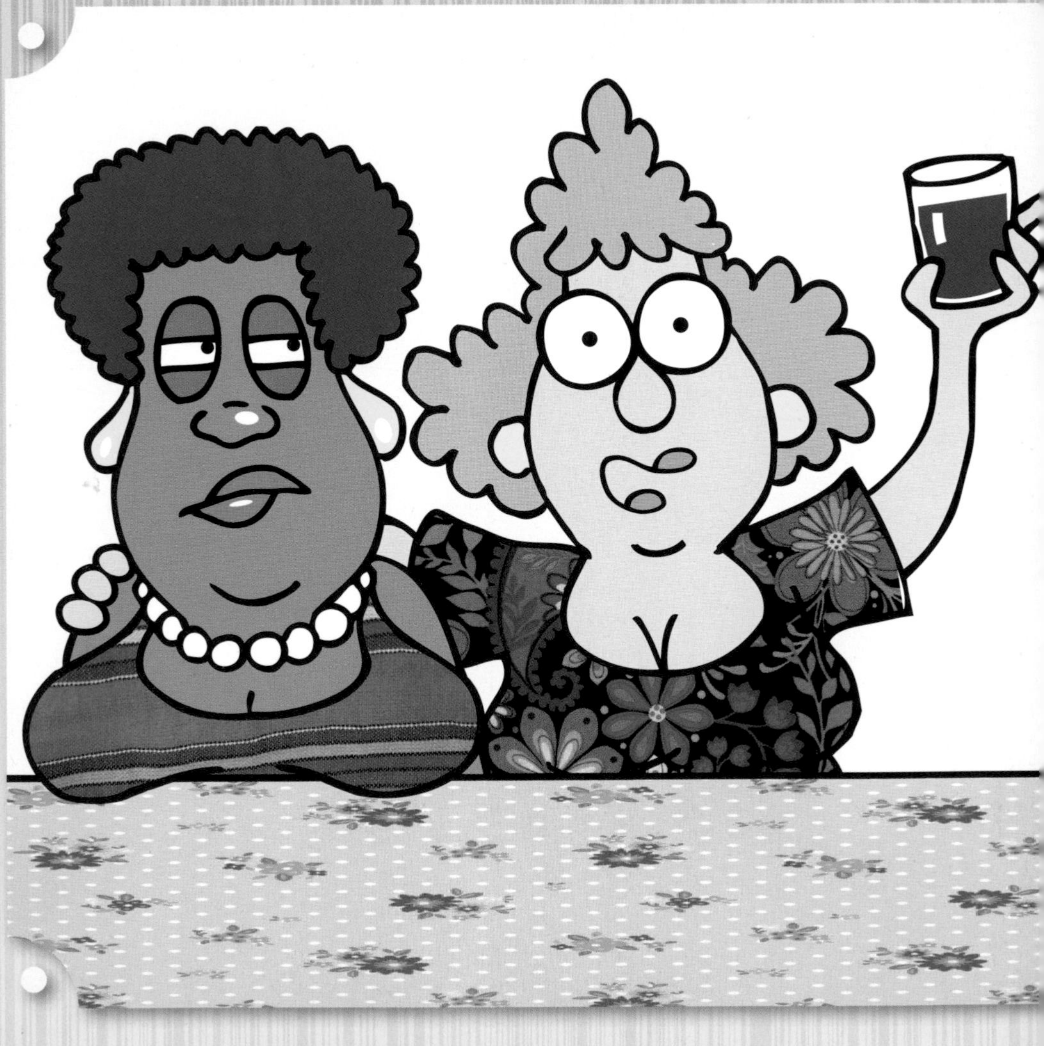

Keep your
friends
close
...and your
wine closer!

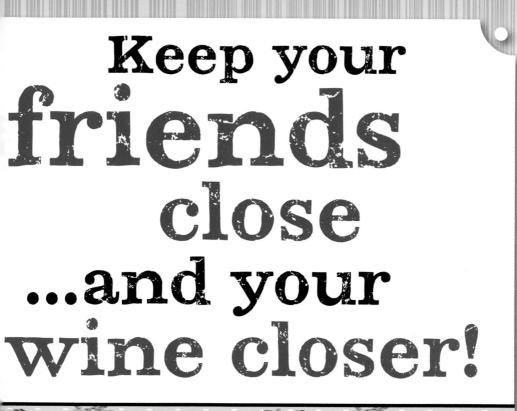

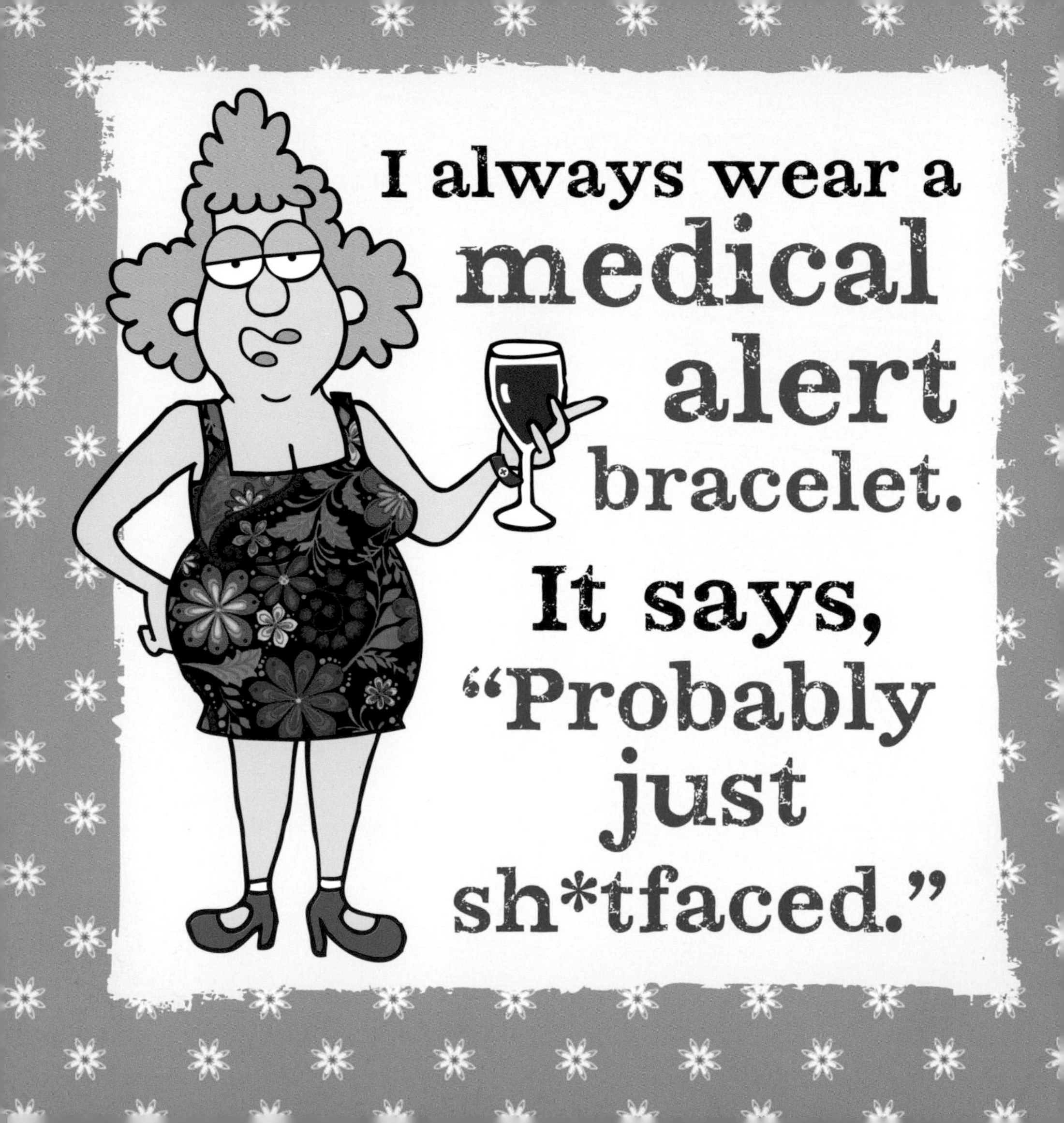

I always wear a
medical
alert
bracelet.
It says,
"Probably
just
sh*tfaced."

I'm so old,

I can remember when vodka only came in vodka flavor.

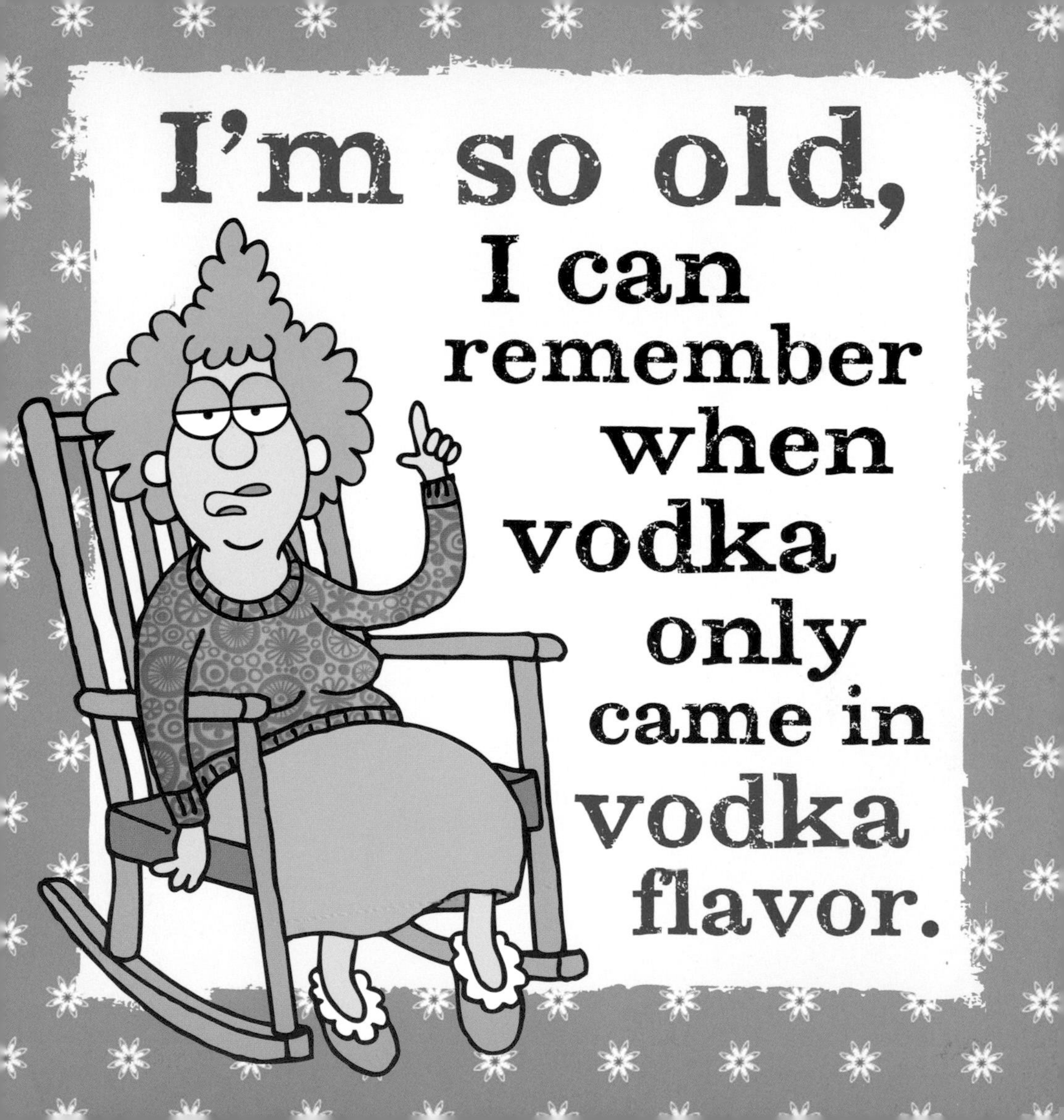

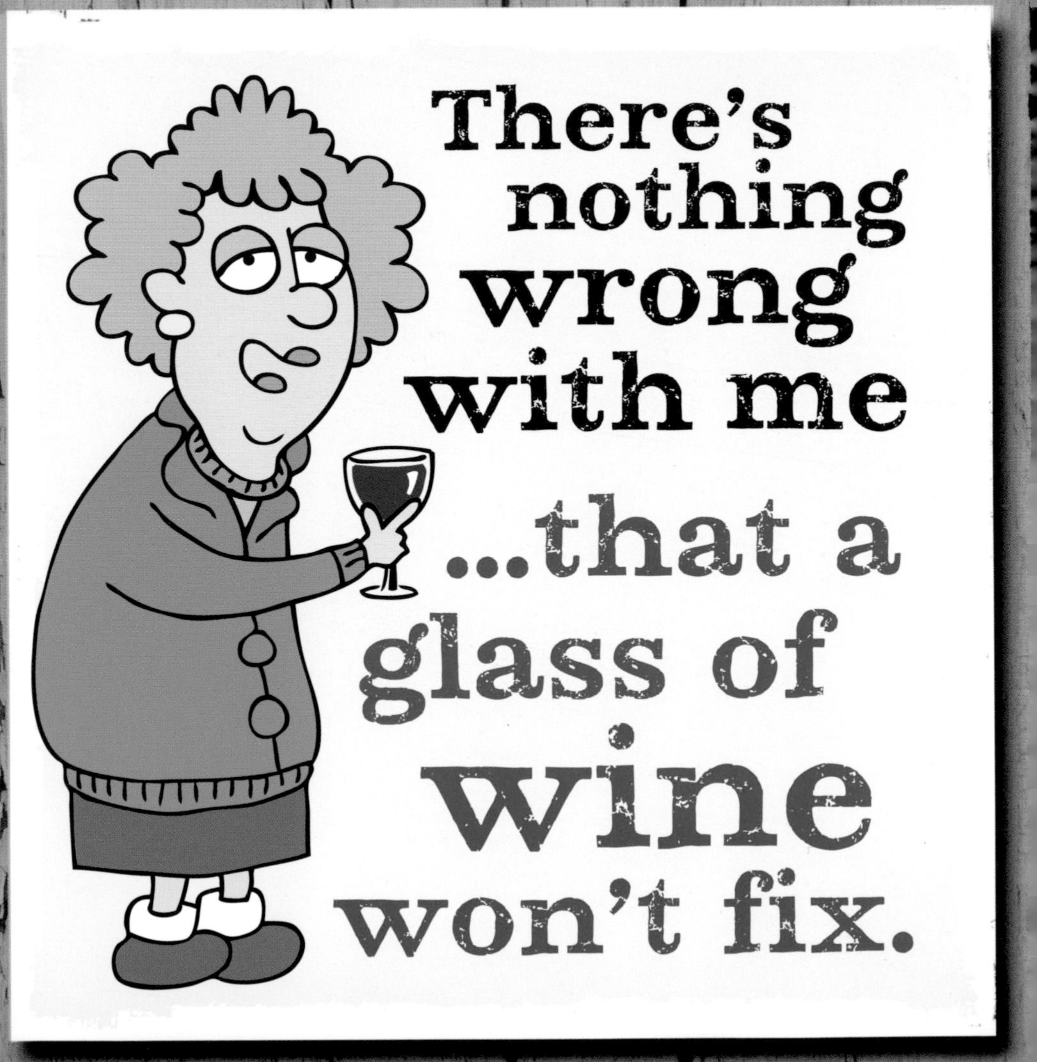
There's nothing wrong with me
...that a glass of wine won't fix.

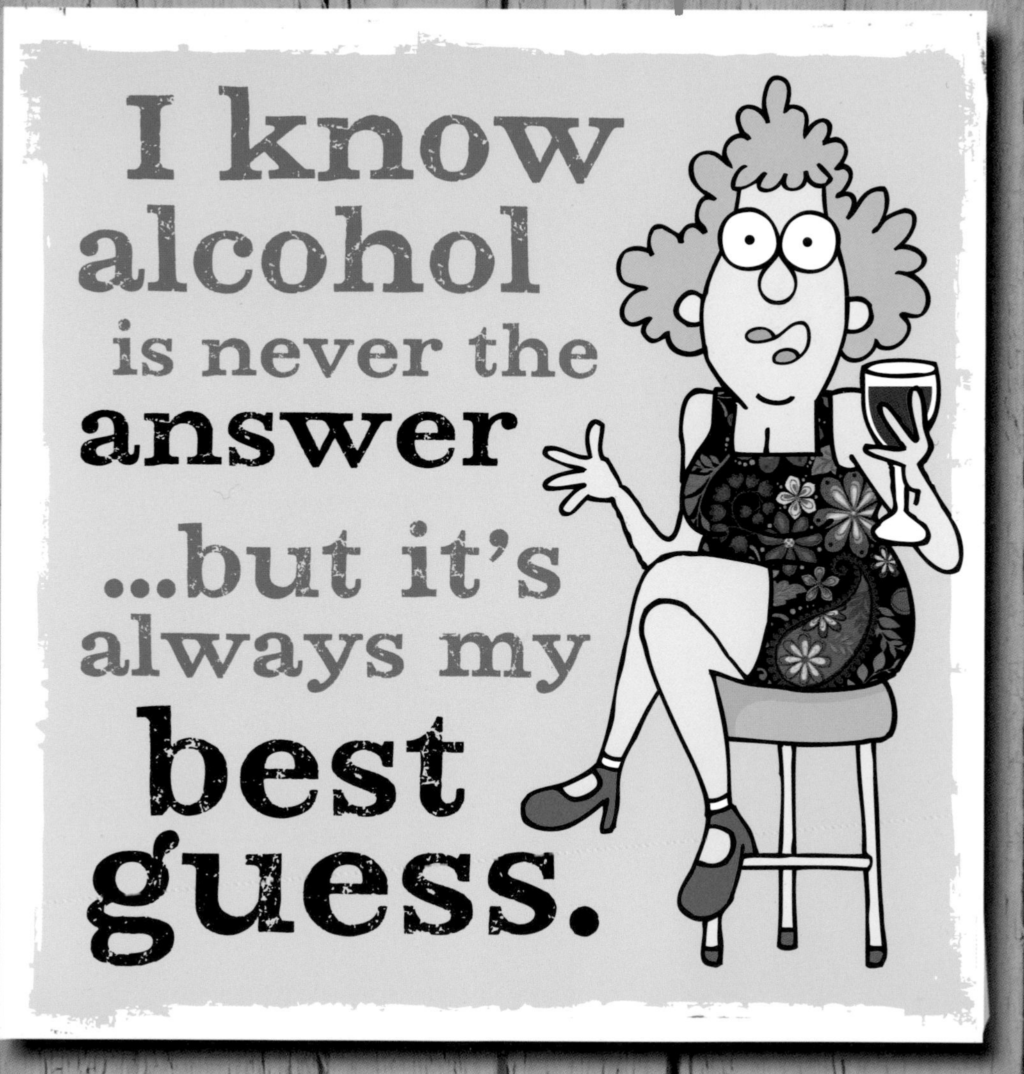
I know
alcohol
is never the
answer
...but it's
always my
best
guess.

Of course, I'll drink more water...

as long as it's frozen and surrounded by alcohol.

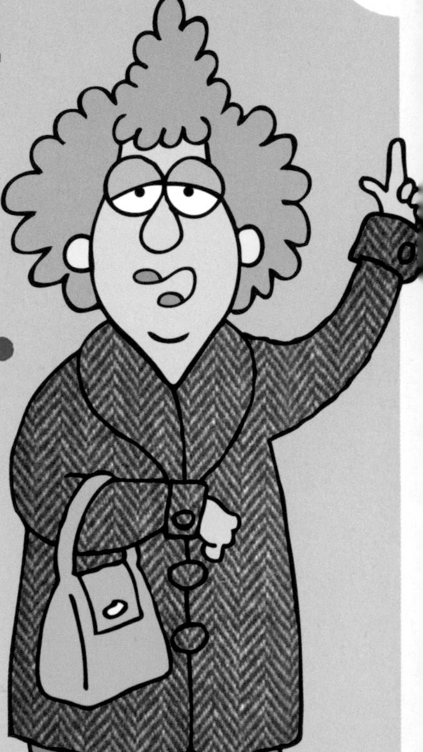

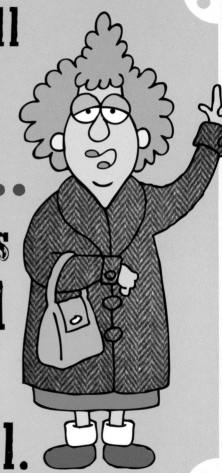

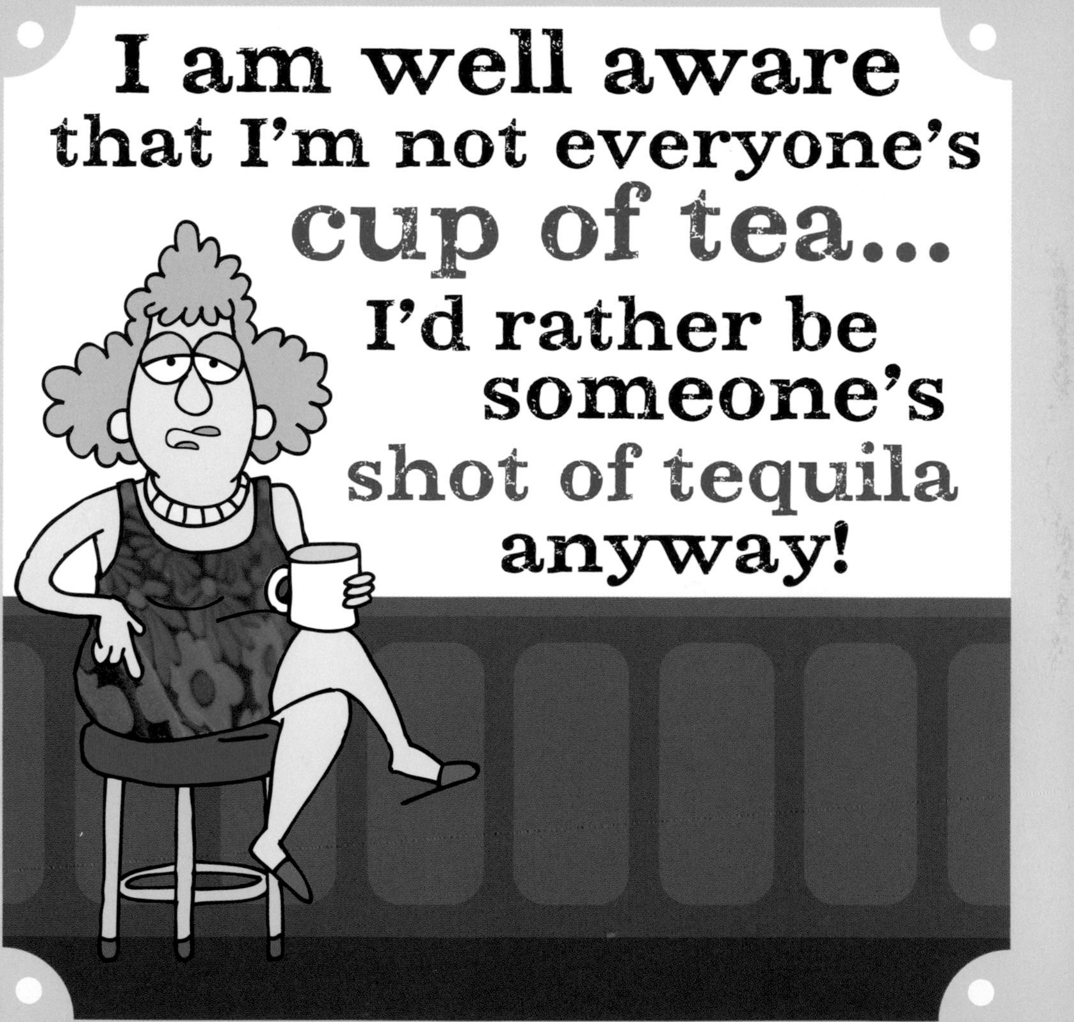
I am well aware
that I'm not everyone's
cup of tea...
I'd rather be
someone's
shot of tequila
anyway!

WISE WORDS ON
GETTING OLD

Technically, if you count up my age in dog years, I'm already dead!

Saying that, I do avoid those all natural "health foods," I need all the freakin' preservatives I can get!

I just wish my head would sort itself out. You see my mind's saying, "I'm in my twenties," and my body is saying, "Yeah YOU wish."

Here's some advice for those of you who like me are over the hill and are now gathering speed as we hurtle down the other side towards that long dirt nap!

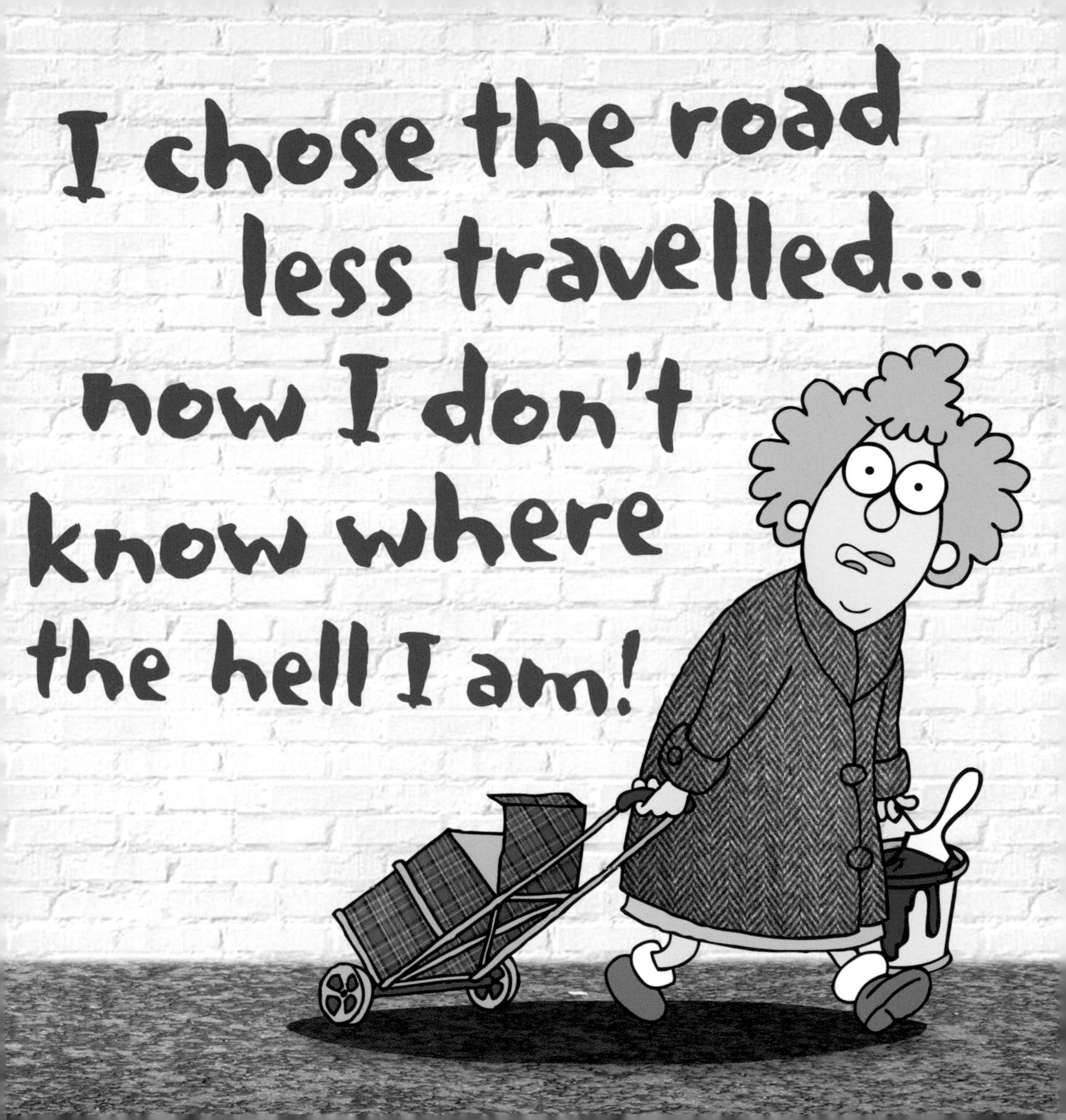
I chose the road less travelled...
now I don't know where the hell I am!

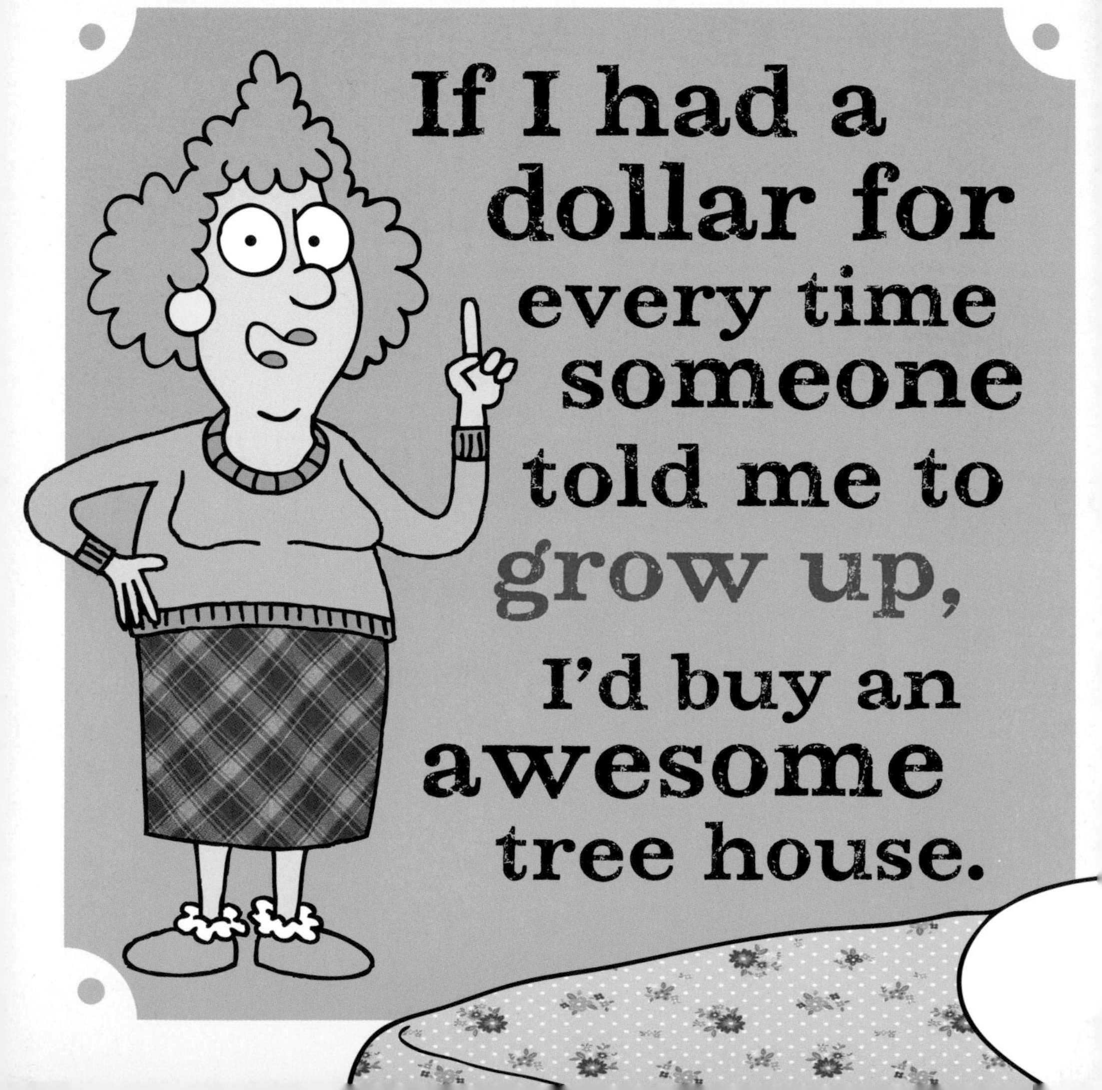
If I had a dollar for every time someone told me to grow up, I'd buy an awesome tree house.

I can still party like a

ROCK STAR.

Unfortunately,
I can't seem to
recover
like one.

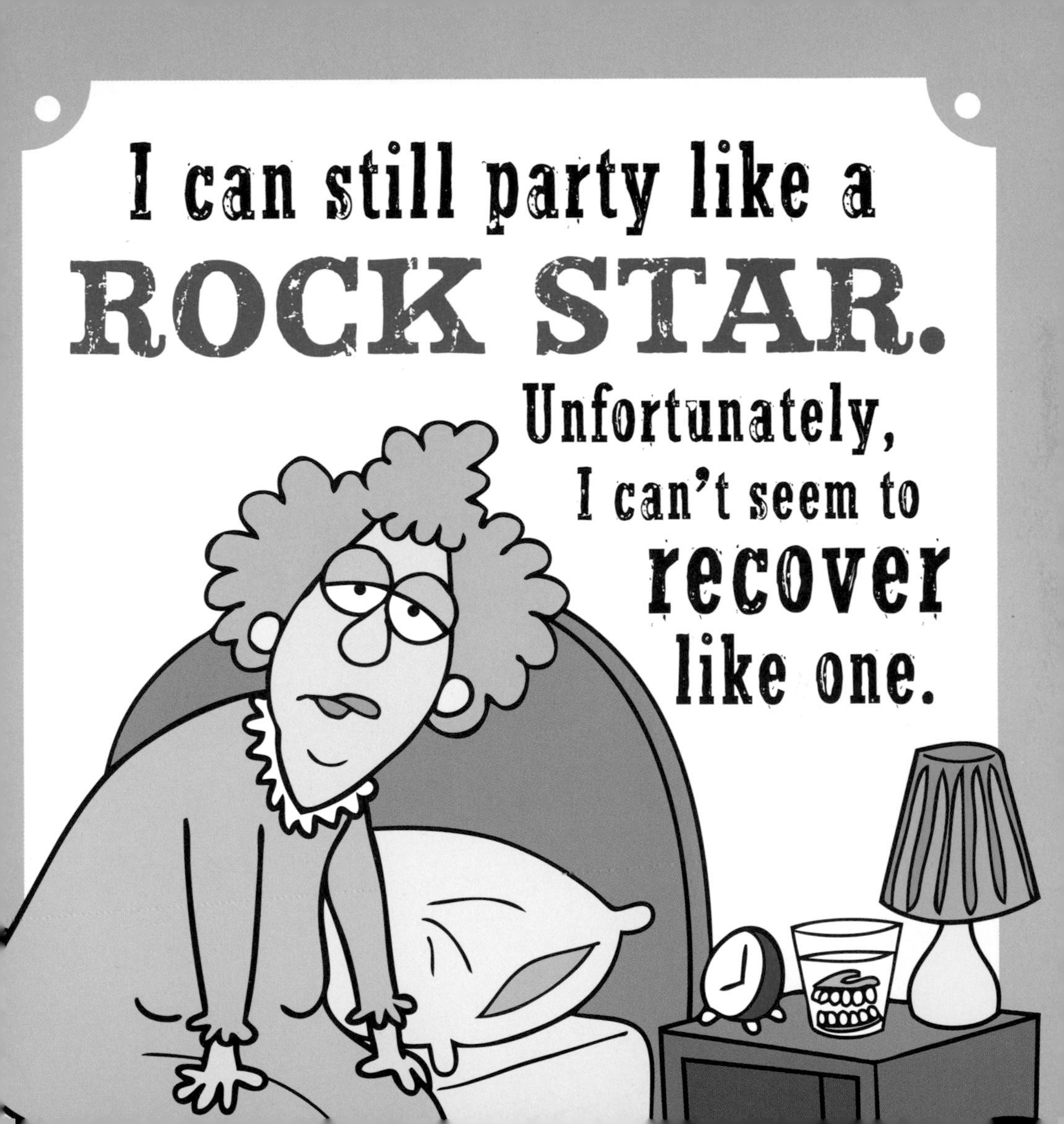

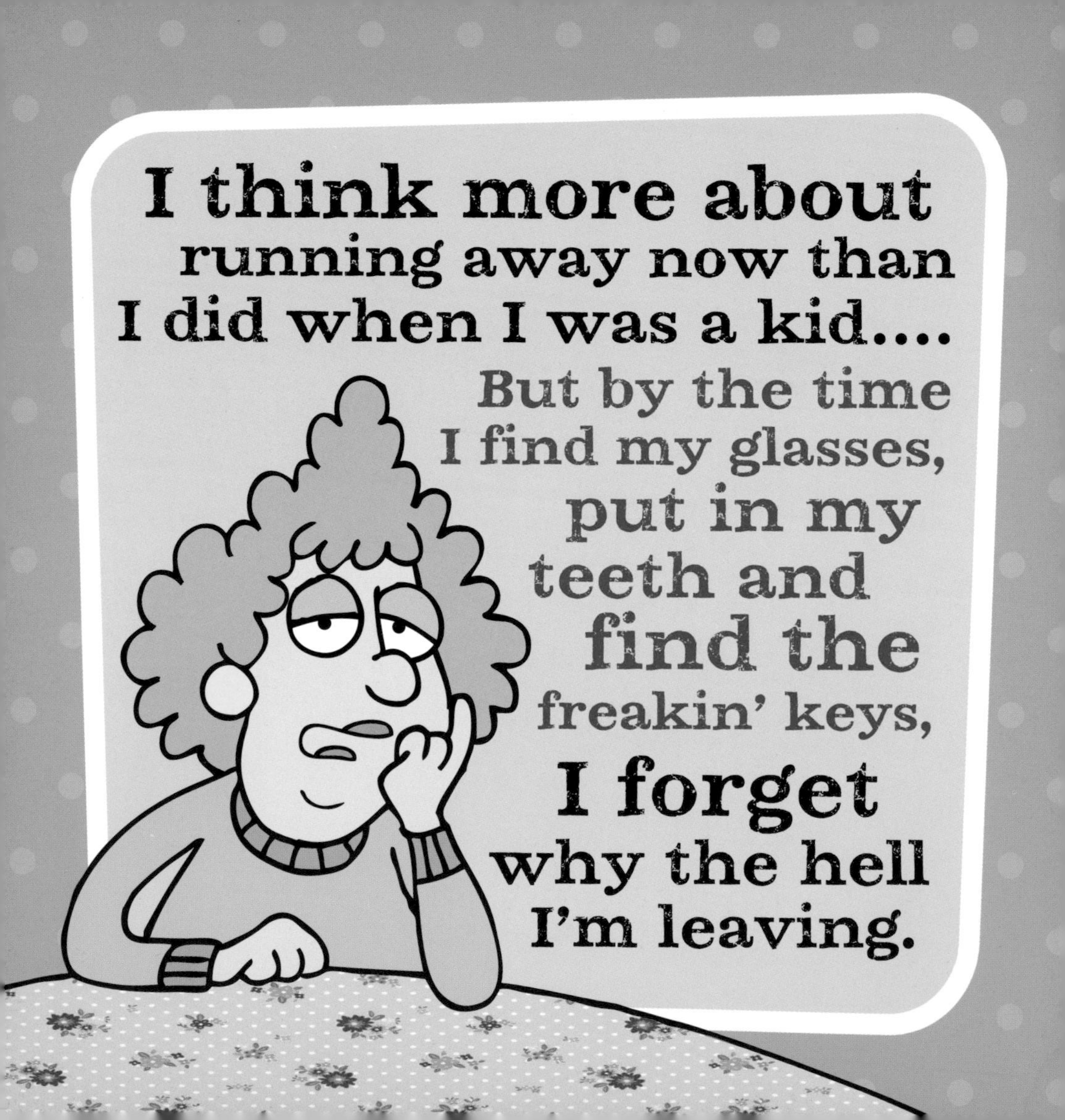
I think more about
running away now than
I did when I was a kid....
But by the time
I find my glasses,
put in my
teeth and
find the
freakin' keys,
I forget
why the hell
I'm leaving.

It's true–
life begins
at 50.

But everything
else starts to
burn out,
spread out
or
fall out.

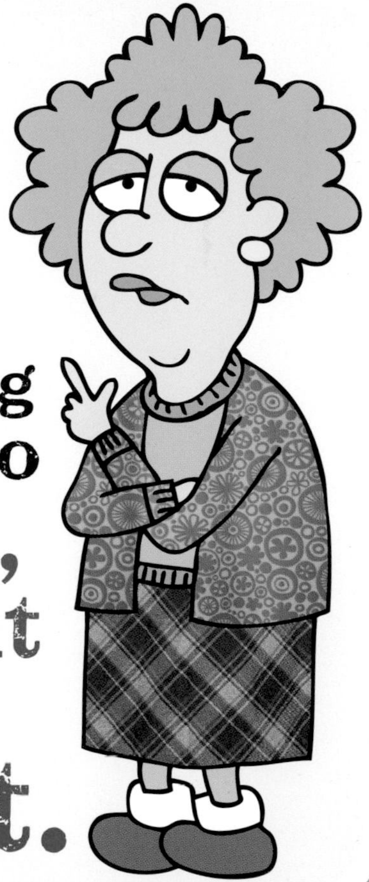

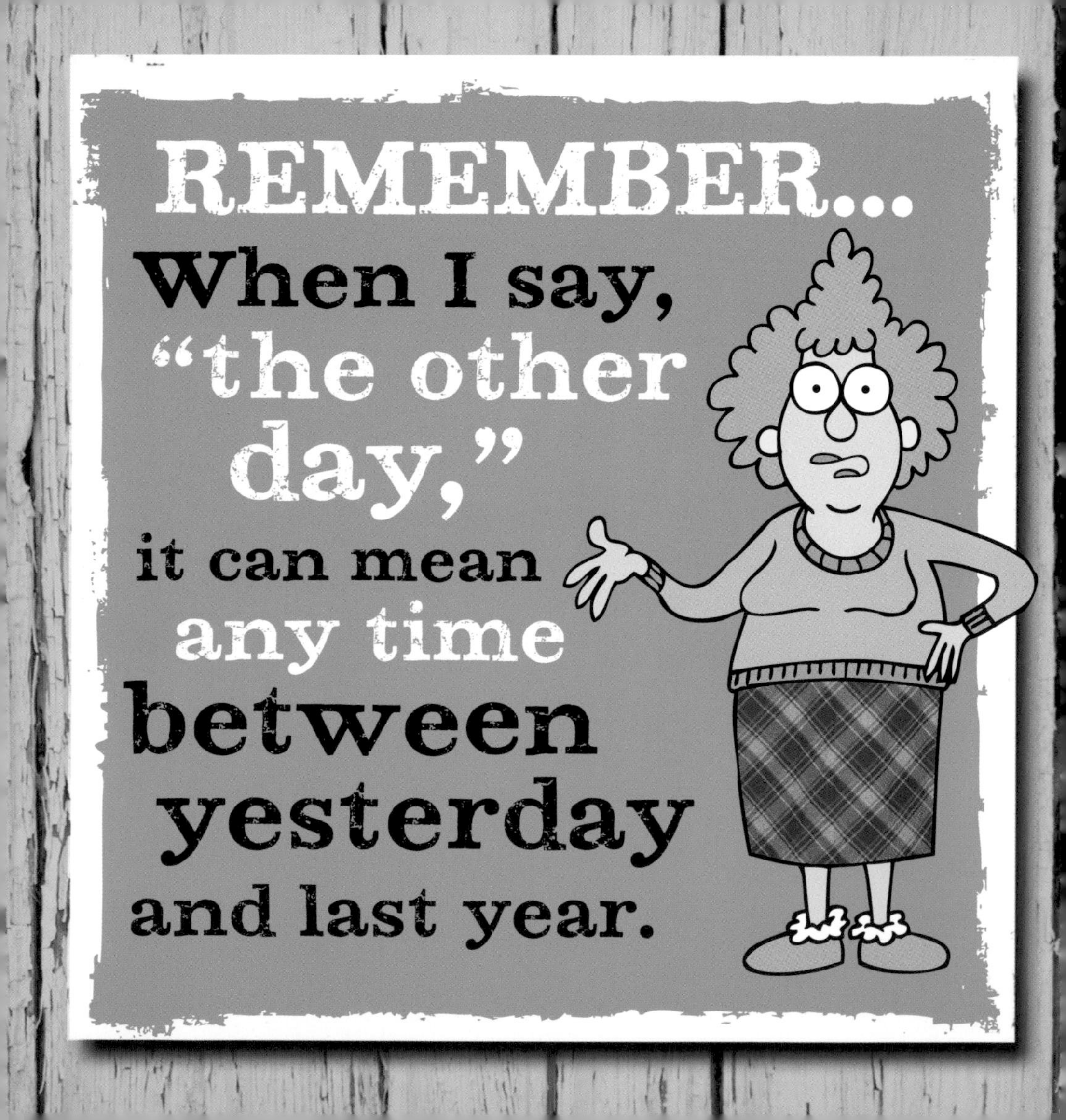
REMEMBER...
When I say,
"the other
day,"
it can mean
any time
between
yesterday
and last year.

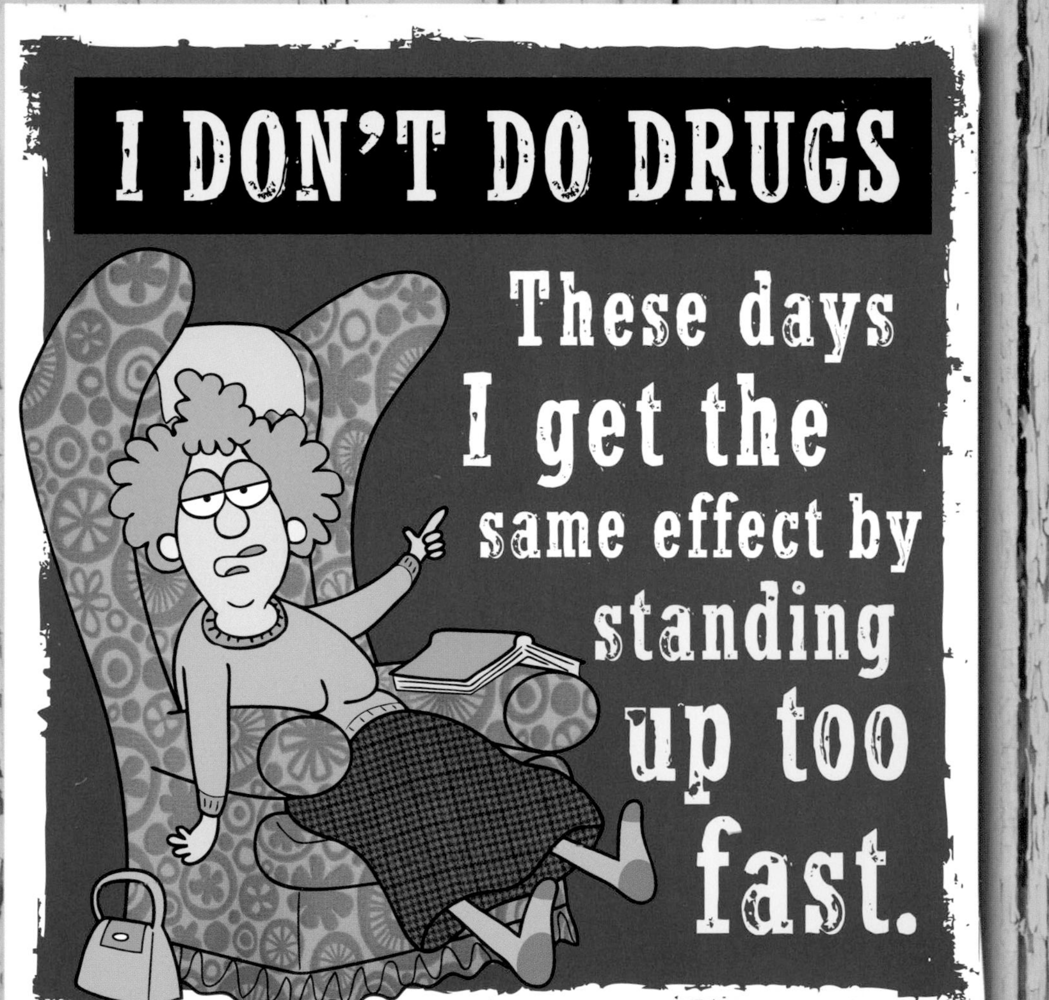
I DON'T DO DRUGS
These days I get the same effect by standing up too fast.

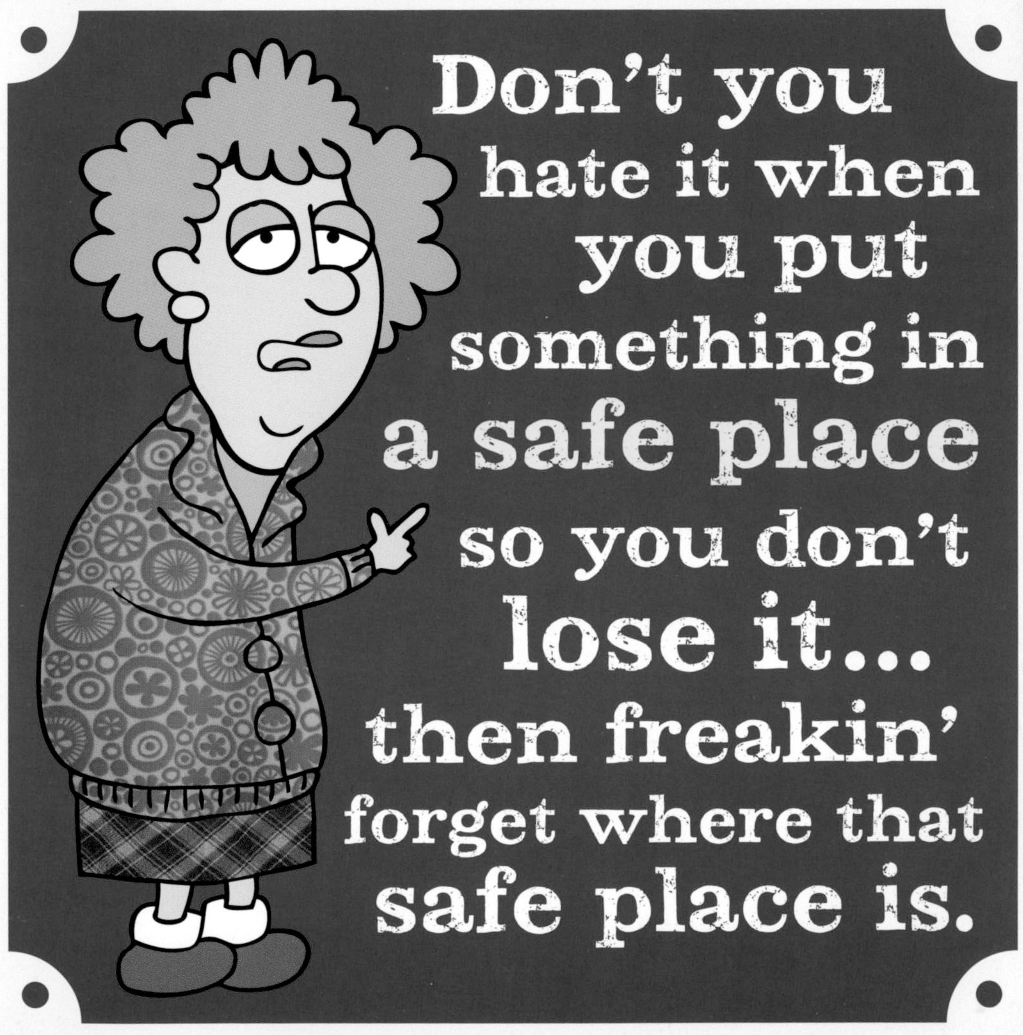

Don't you hate it when you put something in a safe place so you don't lose it... then freakin' forget where that safe place is.

Men go through 3 stages in life:

1. Drinking from boobs.
2. Looking at boobs.
3. Growing boobs.

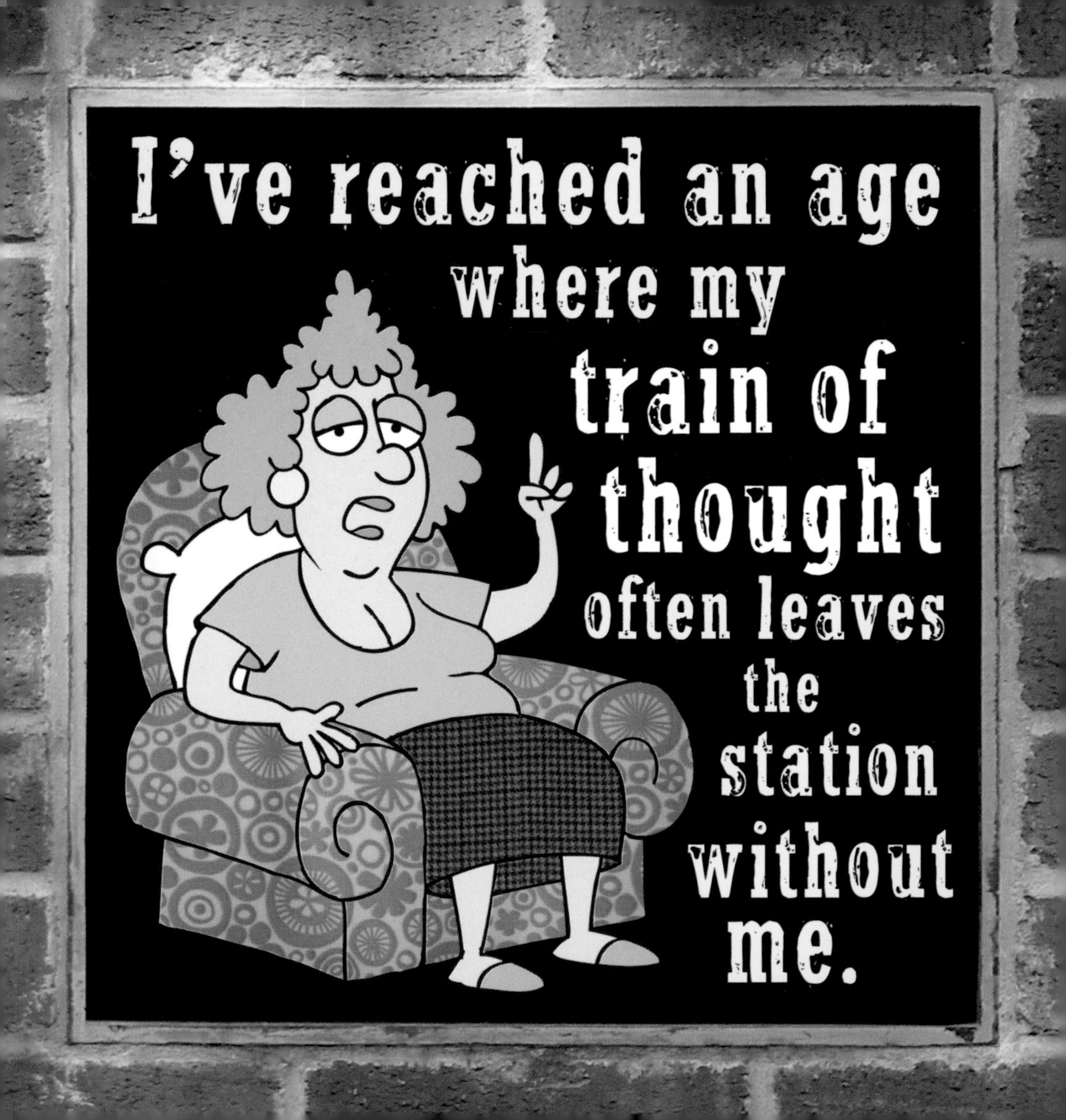
I've reached an age
where my
train of
thought
often leaves
the
station
without
me.

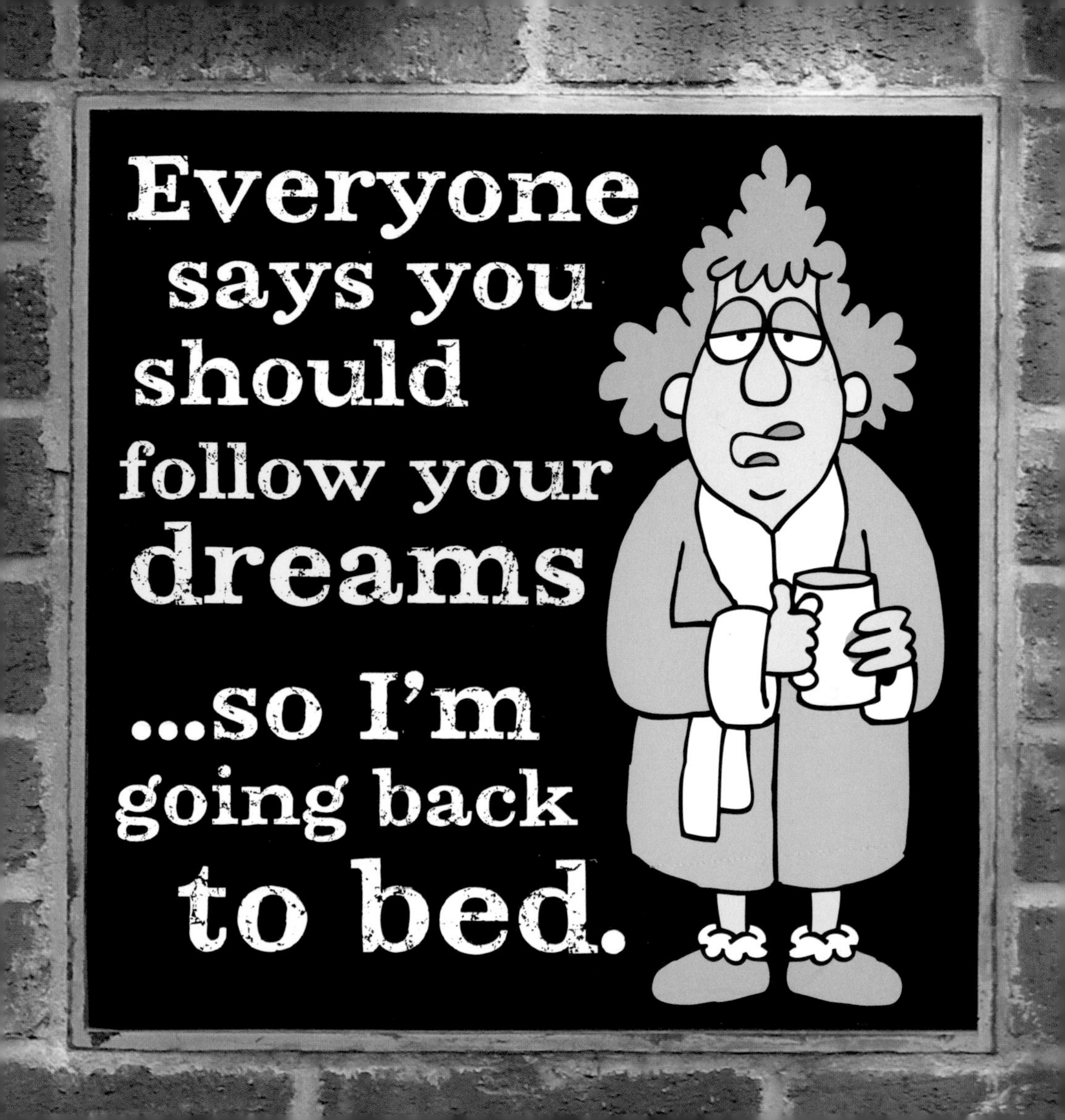
Everyone
says you
should
follow your
dreams
...so I'm
going back
to bed.

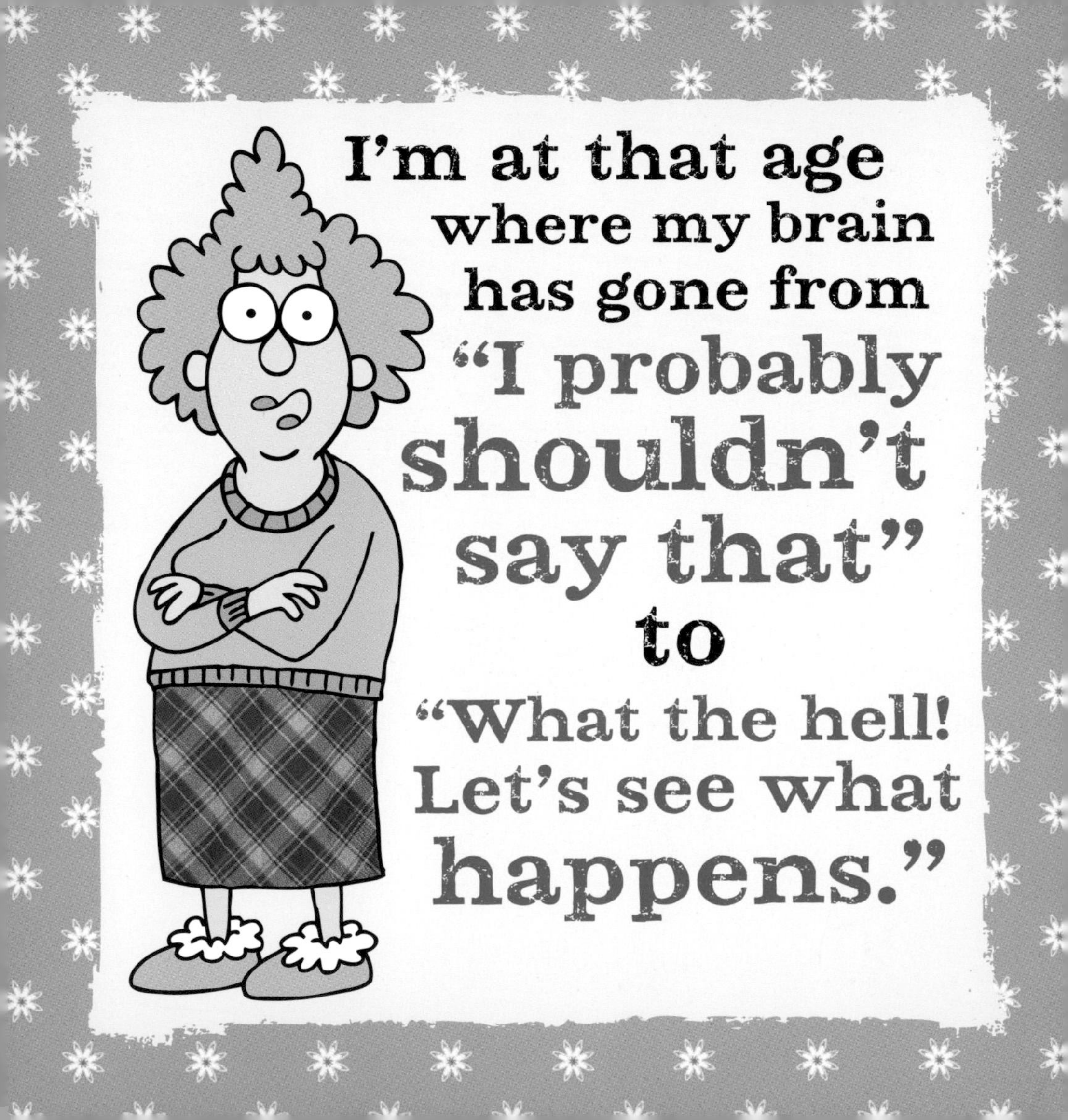

I'm at that age where my brain has gone from "I probably shouldn't say that" to "What the hell! Let's see what happens."

When you're a child, you make funny faces at the mirror.

In middle age, the mirror gets even.

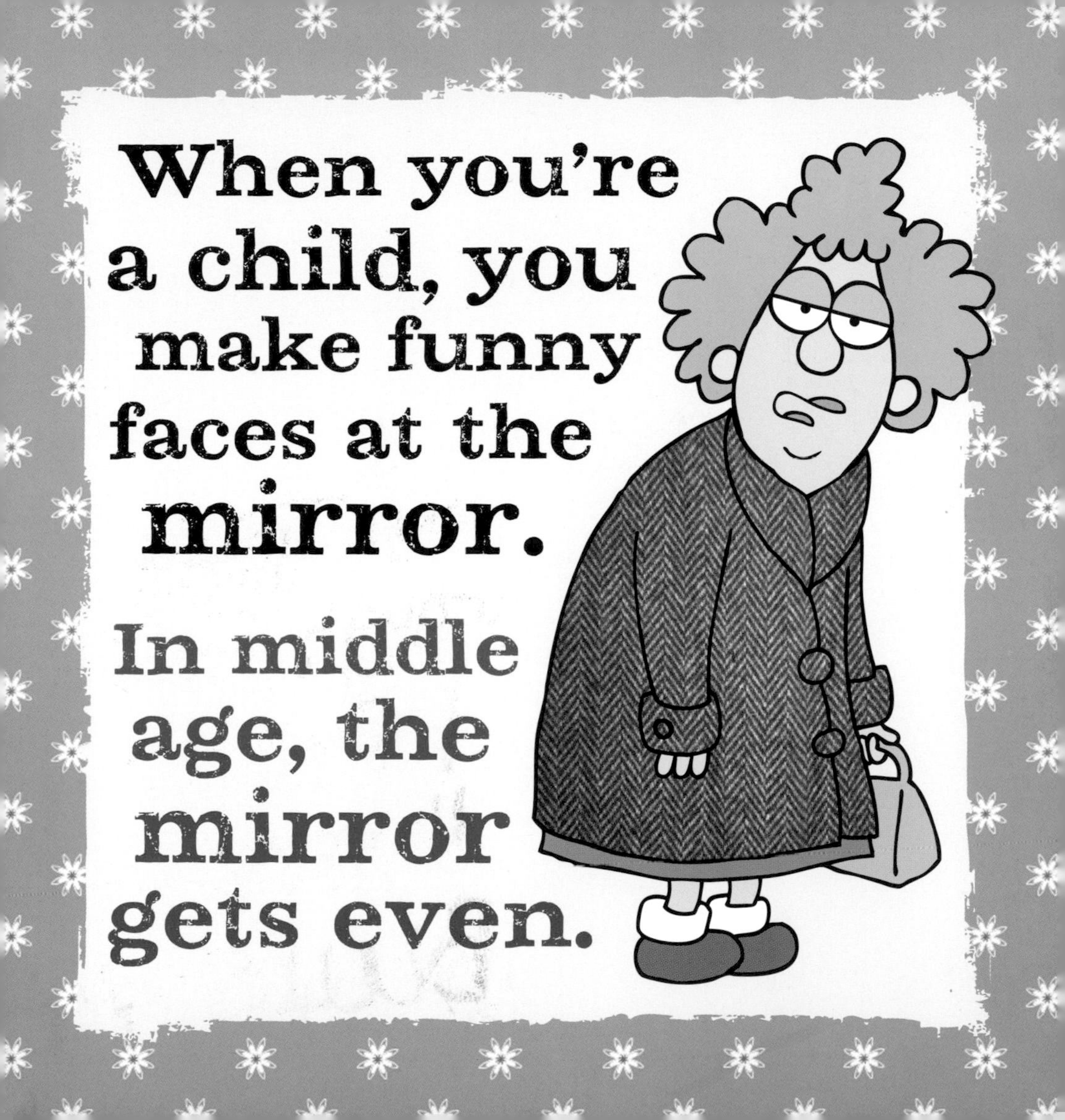

People say,

60 is the new 40.

I hope the cop who just pulled me over agrees.

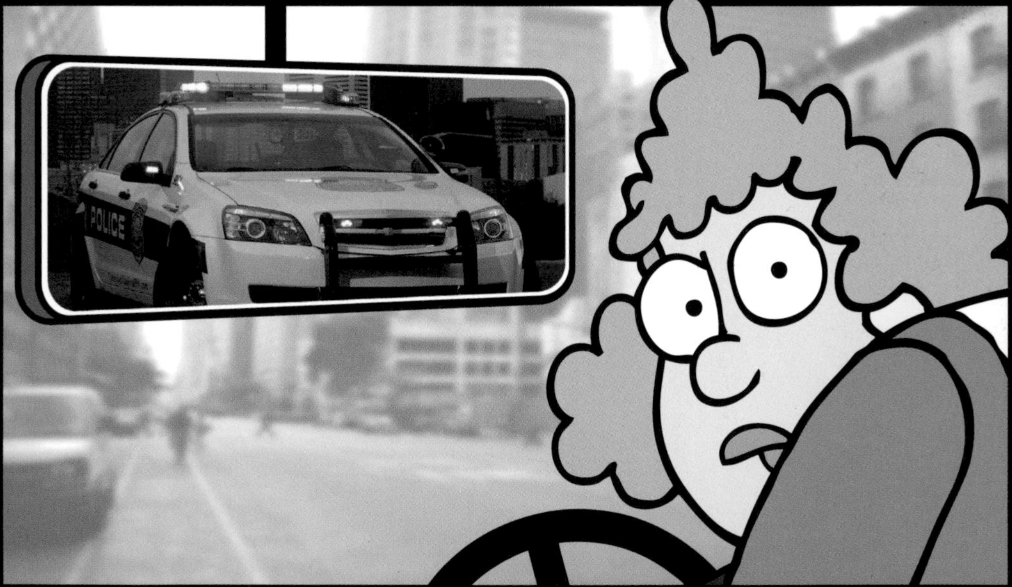
POLICE

I used to **wake up feeling like a million dollars.**

...These days I feel like a bounced check.

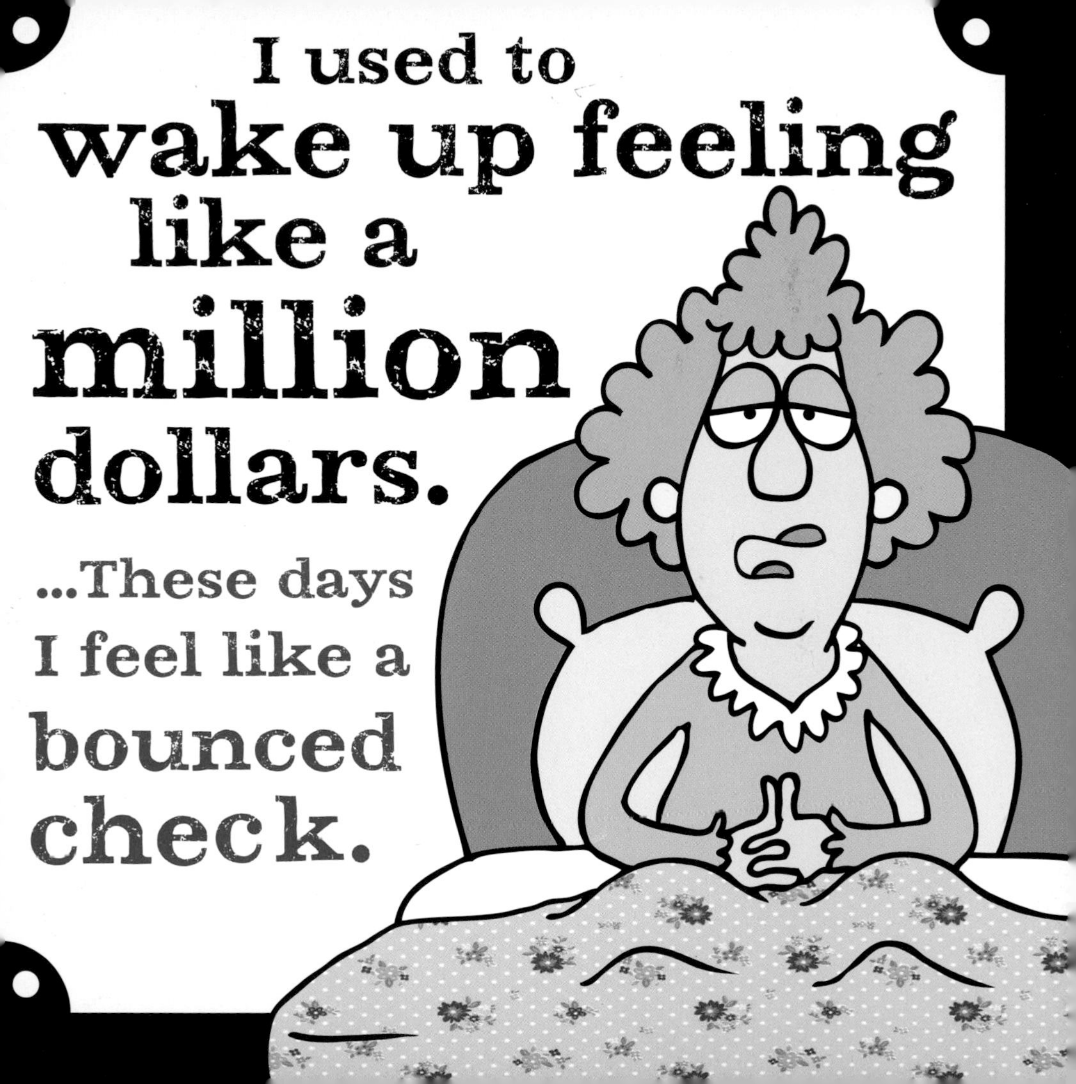

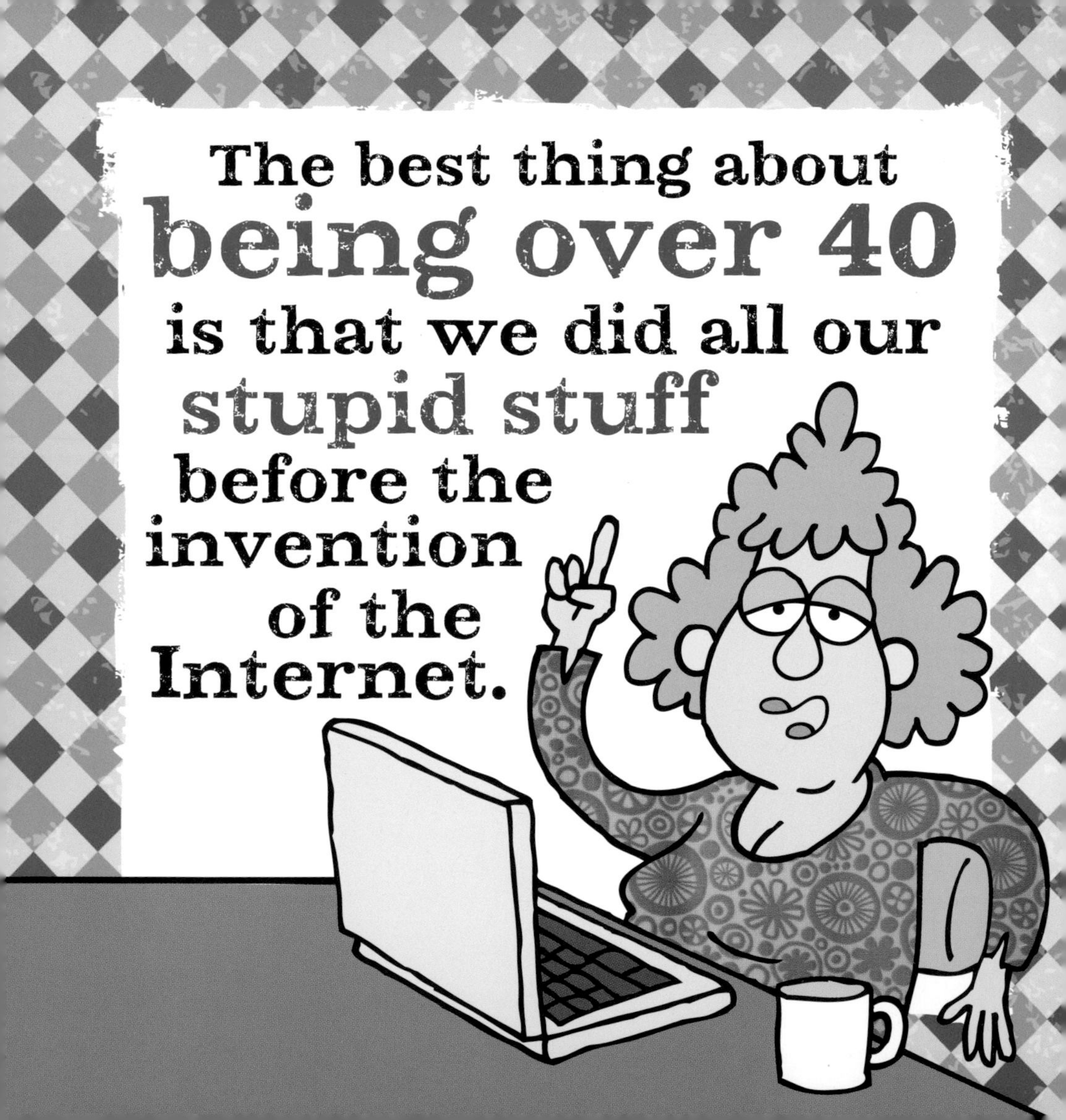
The best thing about
being over 40
is that we did all our
stupid stuff
before the
invention
of the
Internet.

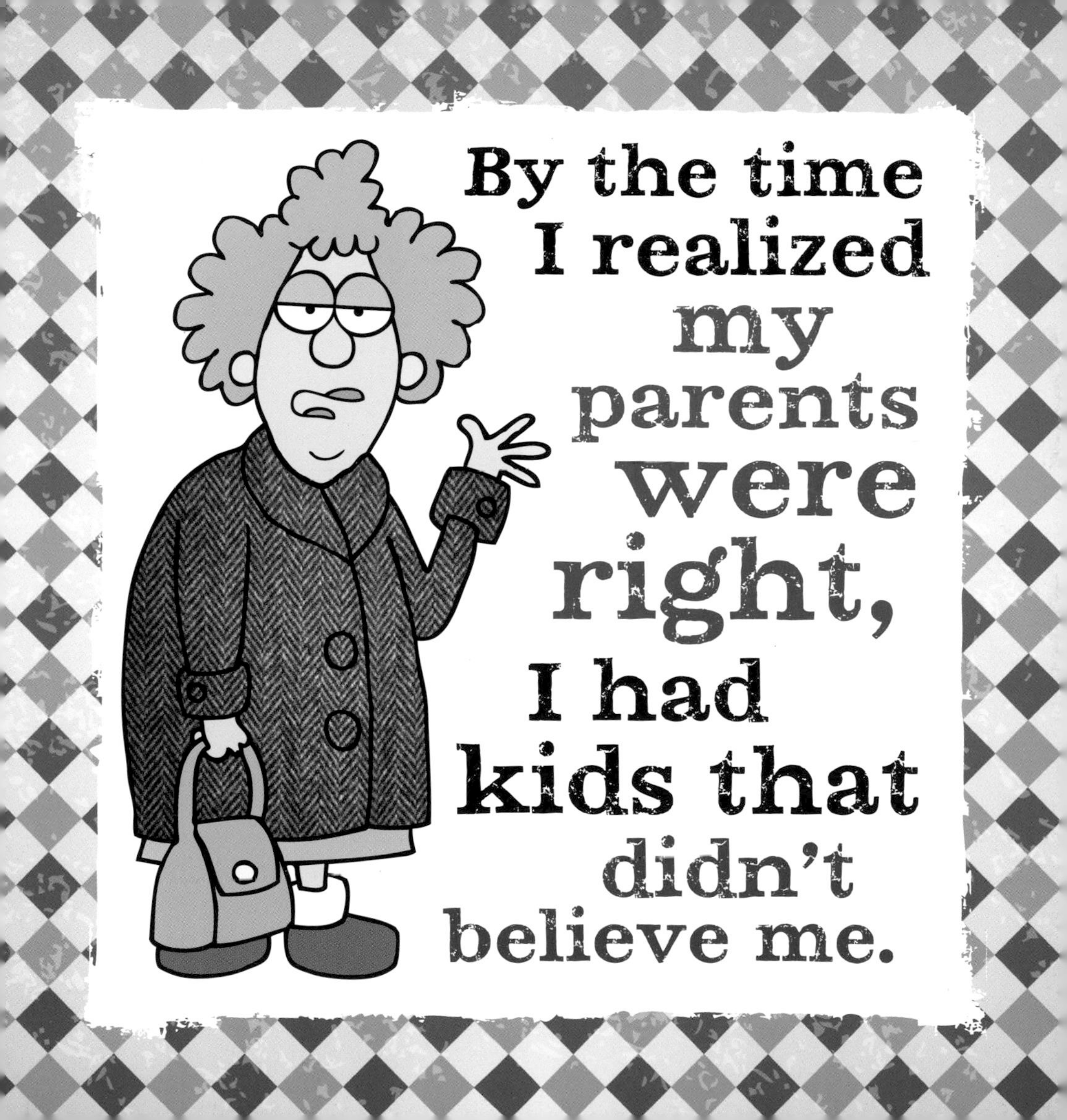

By the time I realized my parents were right, I had kids that didn't believe me.

You know that amazing feeling when you get into bed and go straight to sleep, then wake up in the morning feeling fully refreshed and raring to go?

Yeah, me neither.

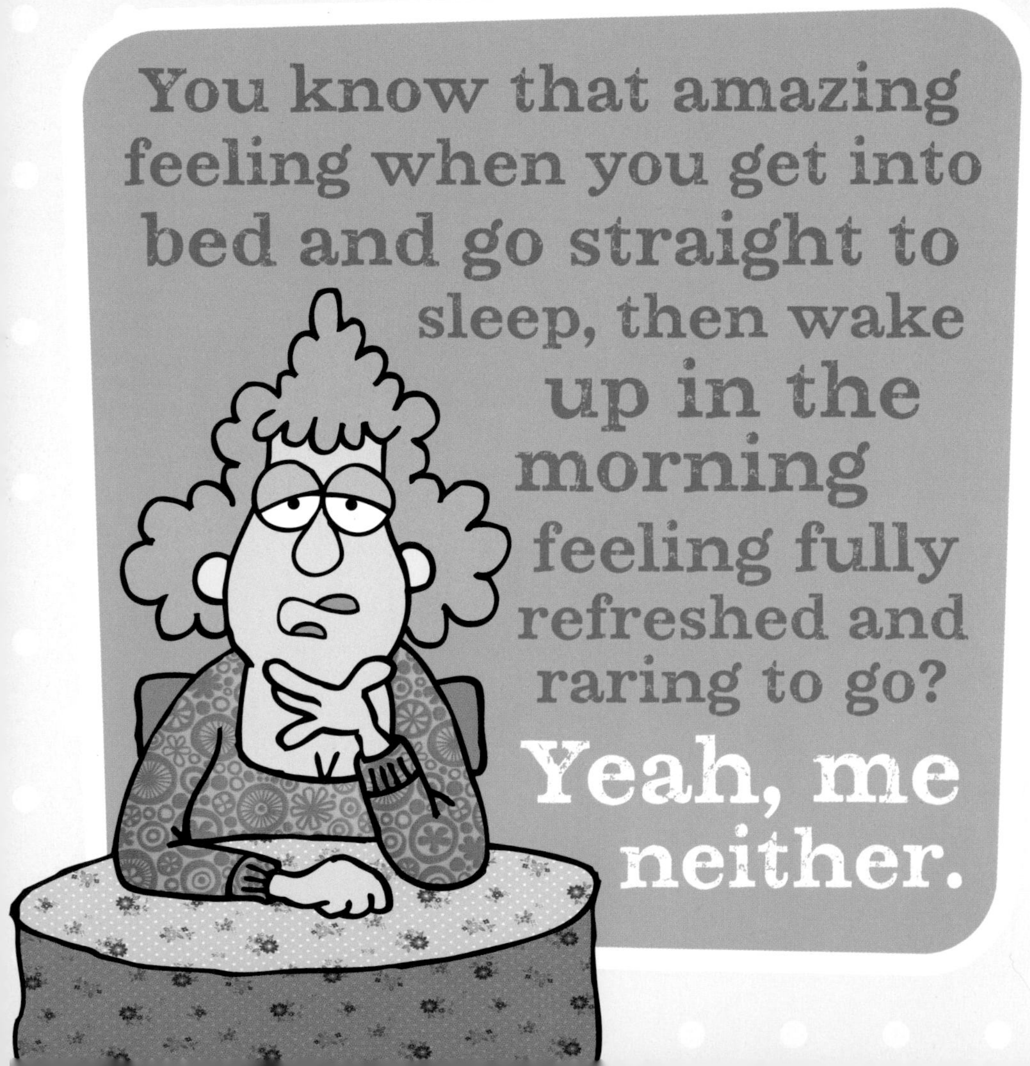

I'm starting to think I'll **never** be old enough to know better.

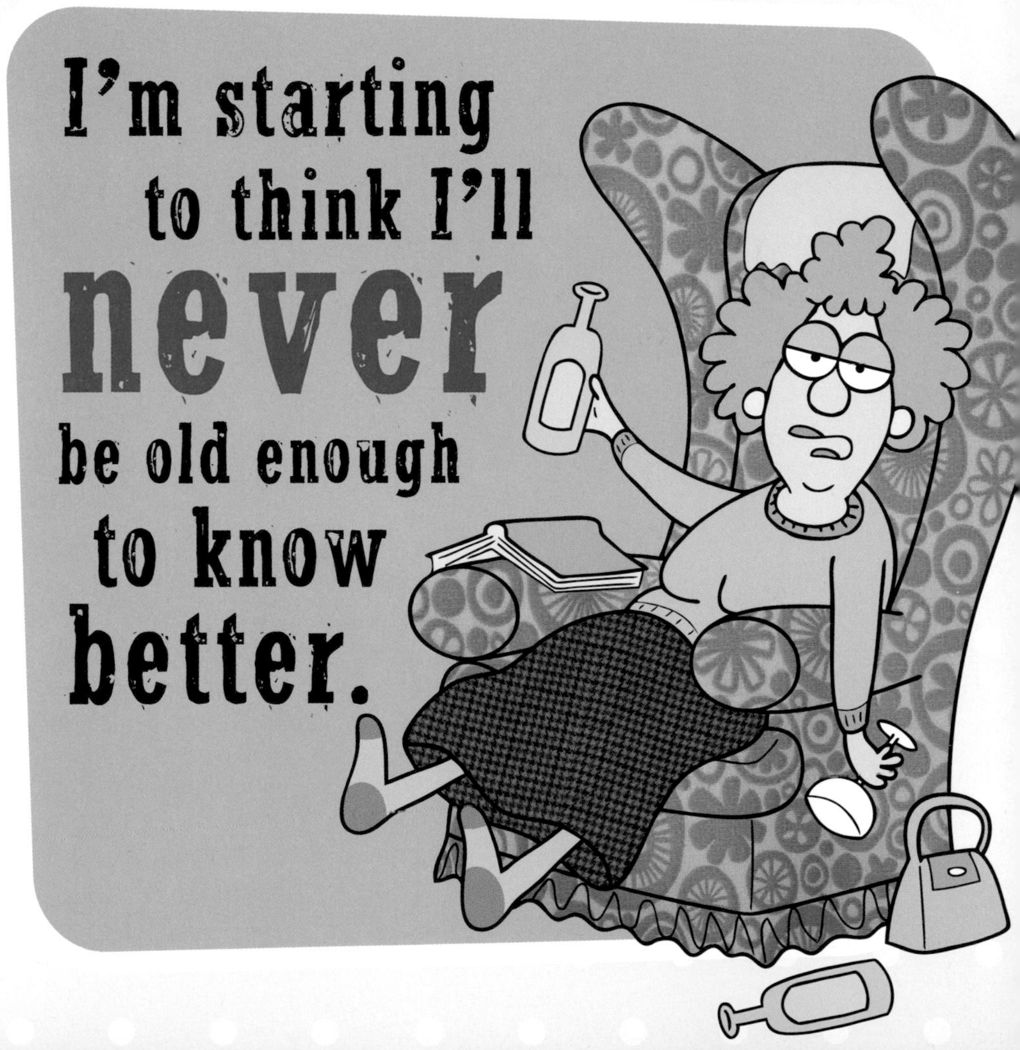

WISE WORDS ON
RELATIONSHIPS

All I want in this life is a little peace, love, understanding... and maybe a chocolate bar the size of my head.

My best advice if you want love and a long-lasting perfect relationship, get yourself a cat or a dog or a pet pig—the last one is my top recommendation.

I've always insisted marriage is like a deck of cards. In the beginning all you need is two hearts and a diamond...and by the end all you need is a club and a spade!

Sure, sometimes I envy my single friends but for the most part I do love my husband, Walt, with all my ass. I'd say heart but my ass is bigger. Read on for more quips and tips on love, marriage and men.

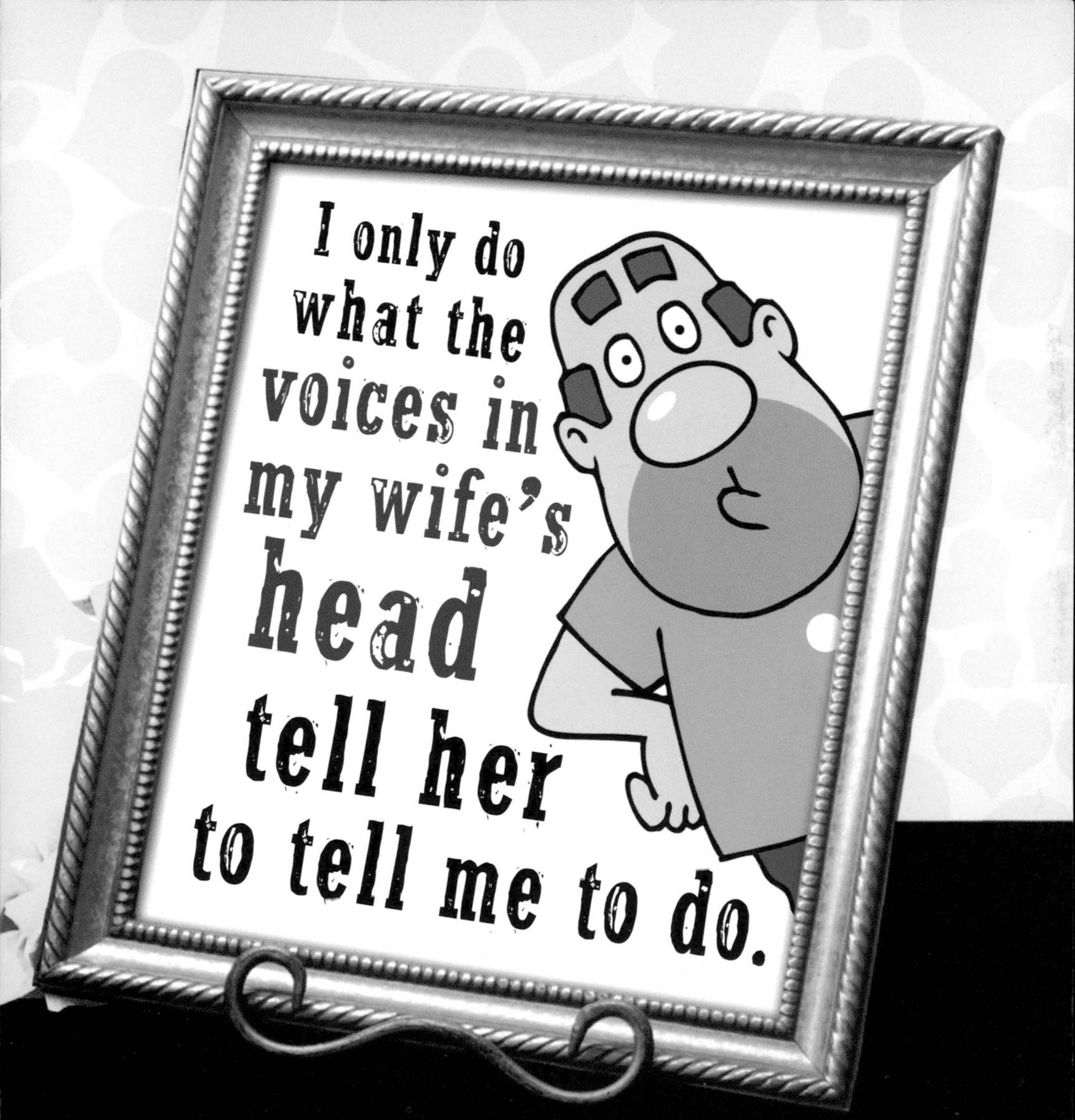
I only do
what the
voices in
my wife's
head
tell her
to tell me to do.

Telling a woman to

calm down

works

about as

well as

trying to

baptize

a cat.

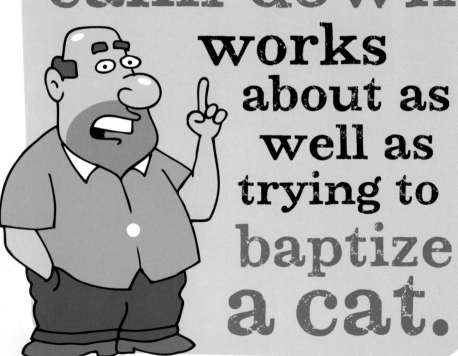

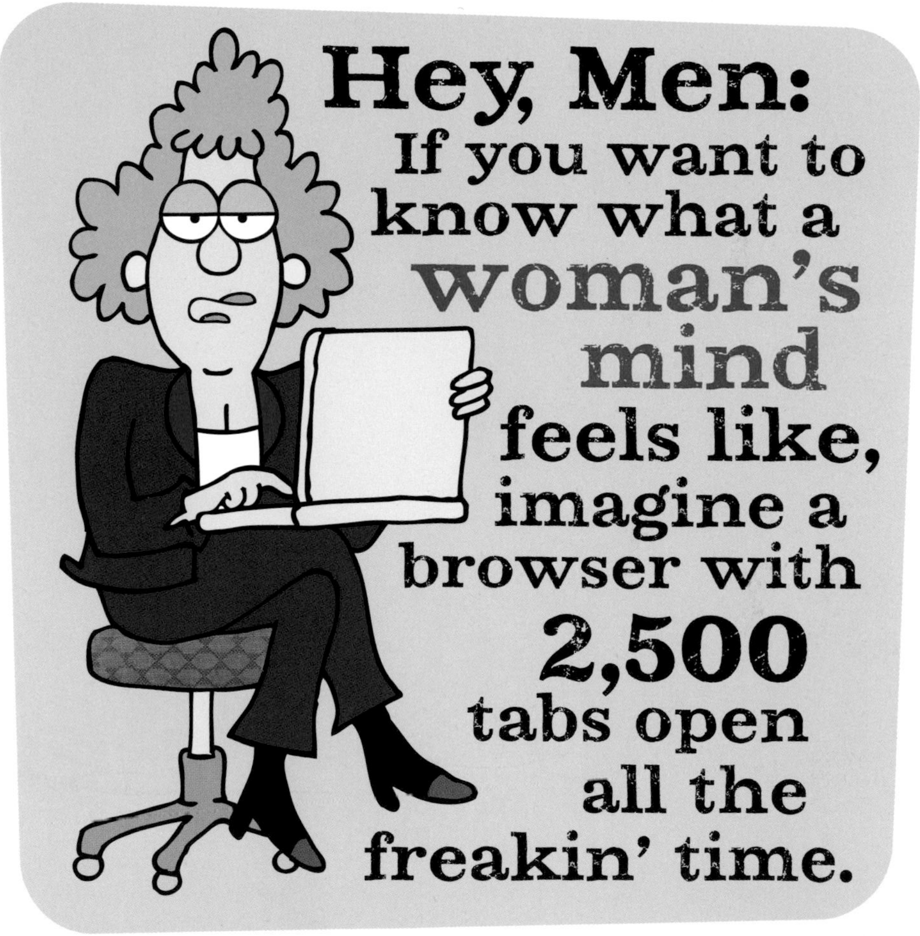
Hey, Men:
If you want to know what a woman's mind feels like, imagine a browser with 2,500 tabs open all the freakin' time.

I was at a wedding reception once where all the married men were asked to "Stand next to the one person who has made your life worth living." The bartender was almost crushed to death.

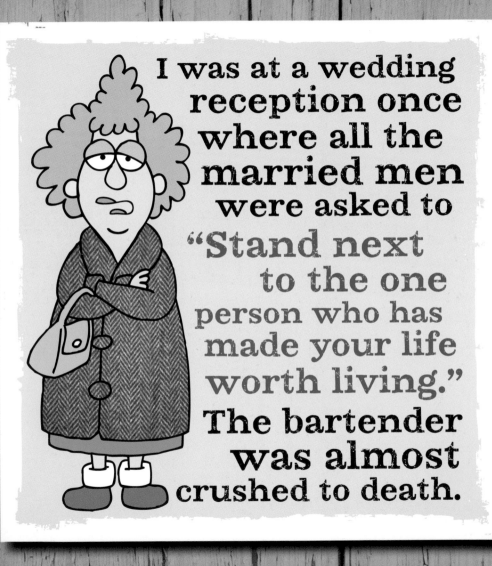

Once in a while
you meet
someone
who makes you
smile when
you think
about them.
Stay away
from them–
they're
trouble!

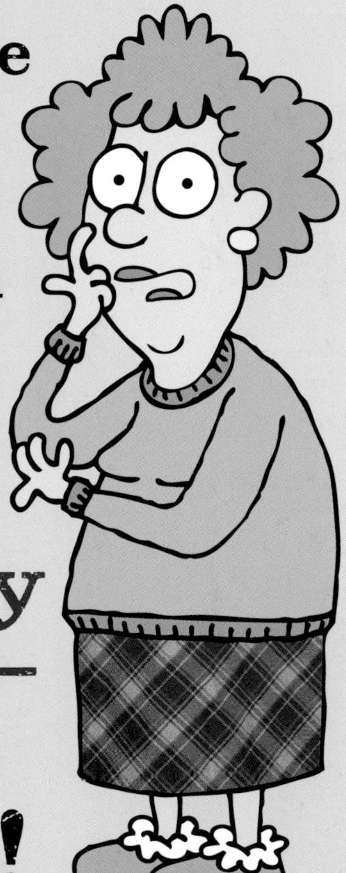

Google is definitely

a woman.

It doesn't
let you
finish a
sentence
without
suggesting
other ideas.

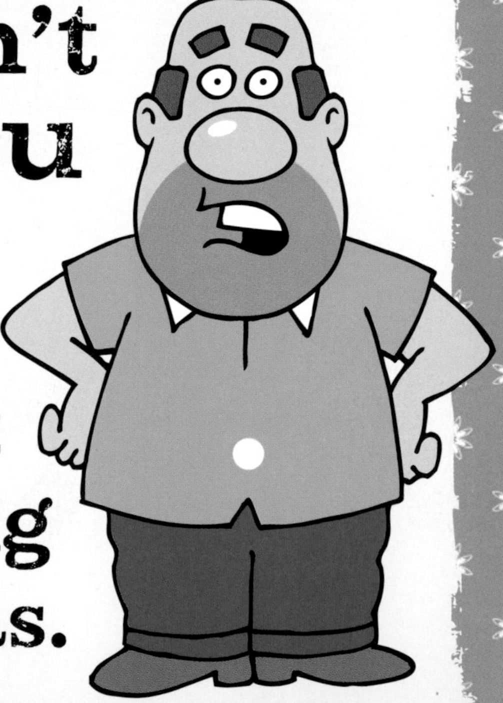

Walt said he wanted
an open
relationship,
so I pushed him
out of an "open"
window.
The funeral will be
an "open" casket
followed by an
"open" bar.

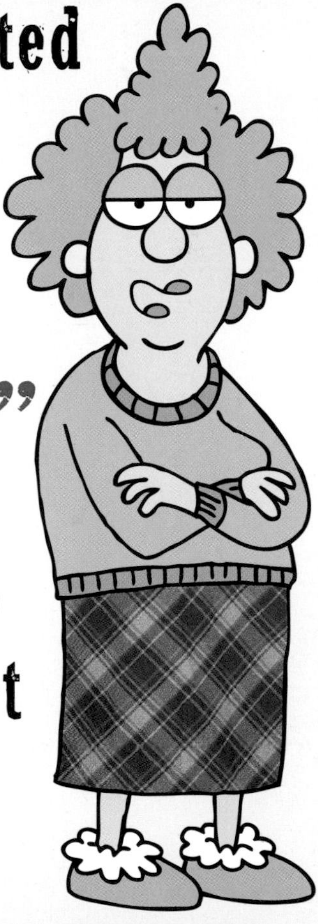

Condoms don't guarantee safe sex anymore.

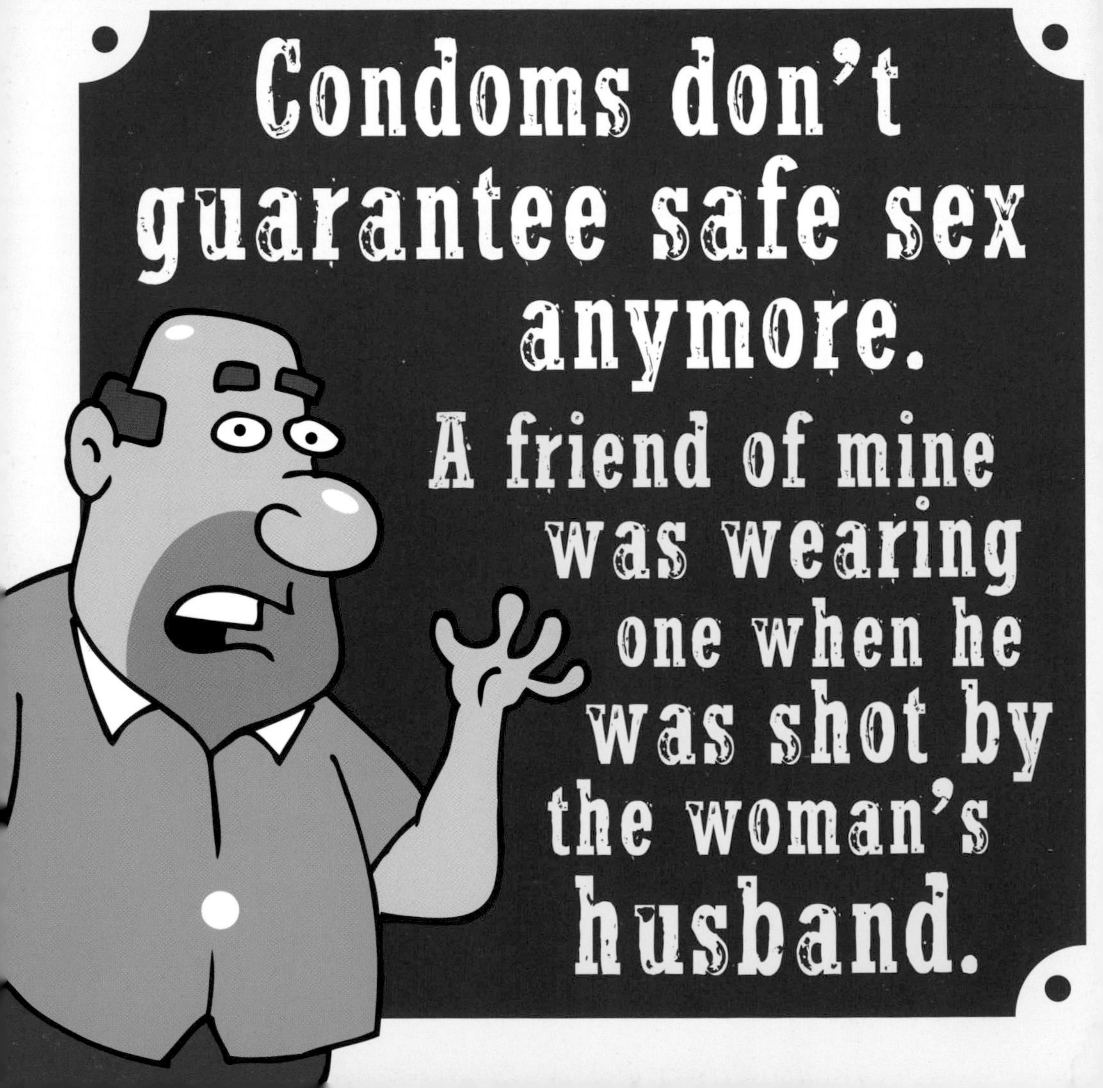

A friend of mine was wearing one when he was shot by the woman's husband.

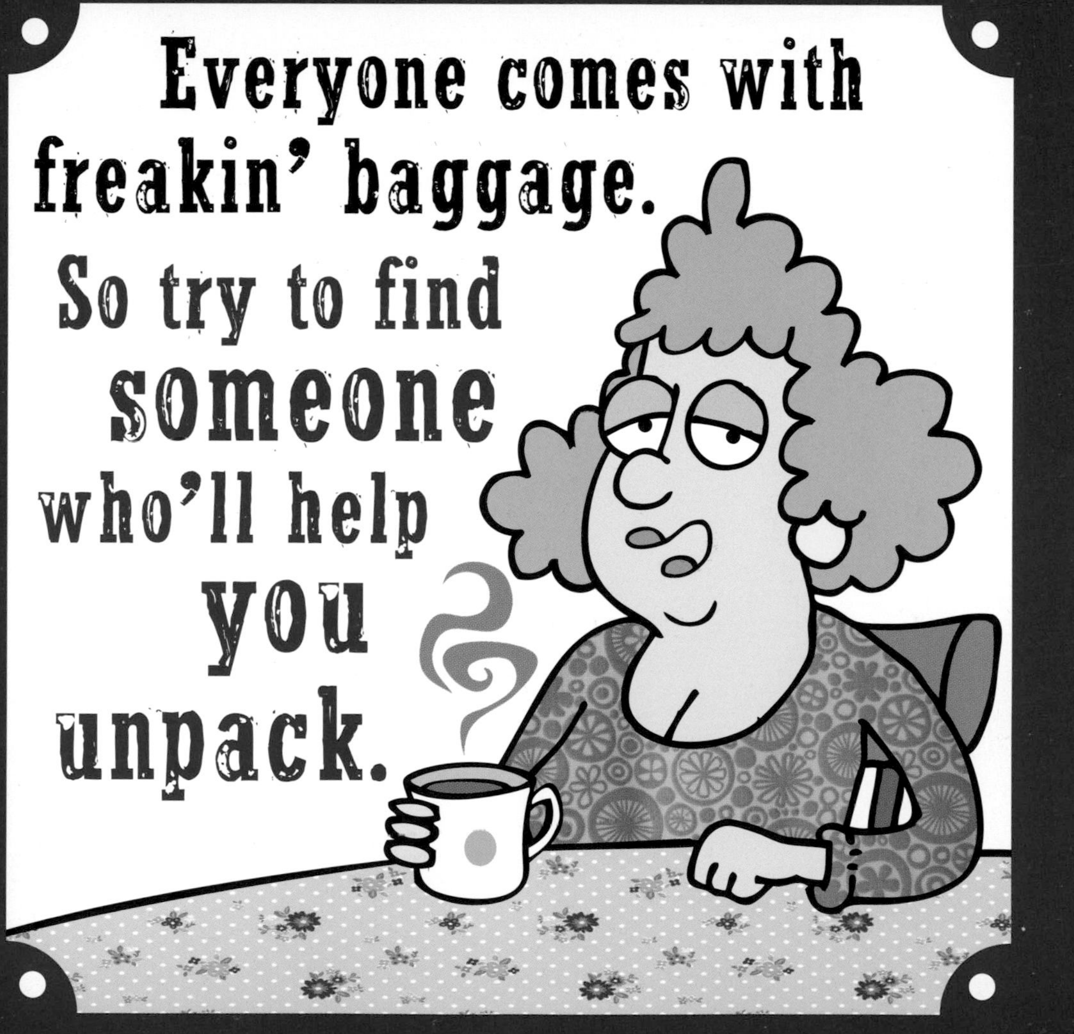
Everyone comes with freakin' baggage.
So try to find someone who'll help you unpack.

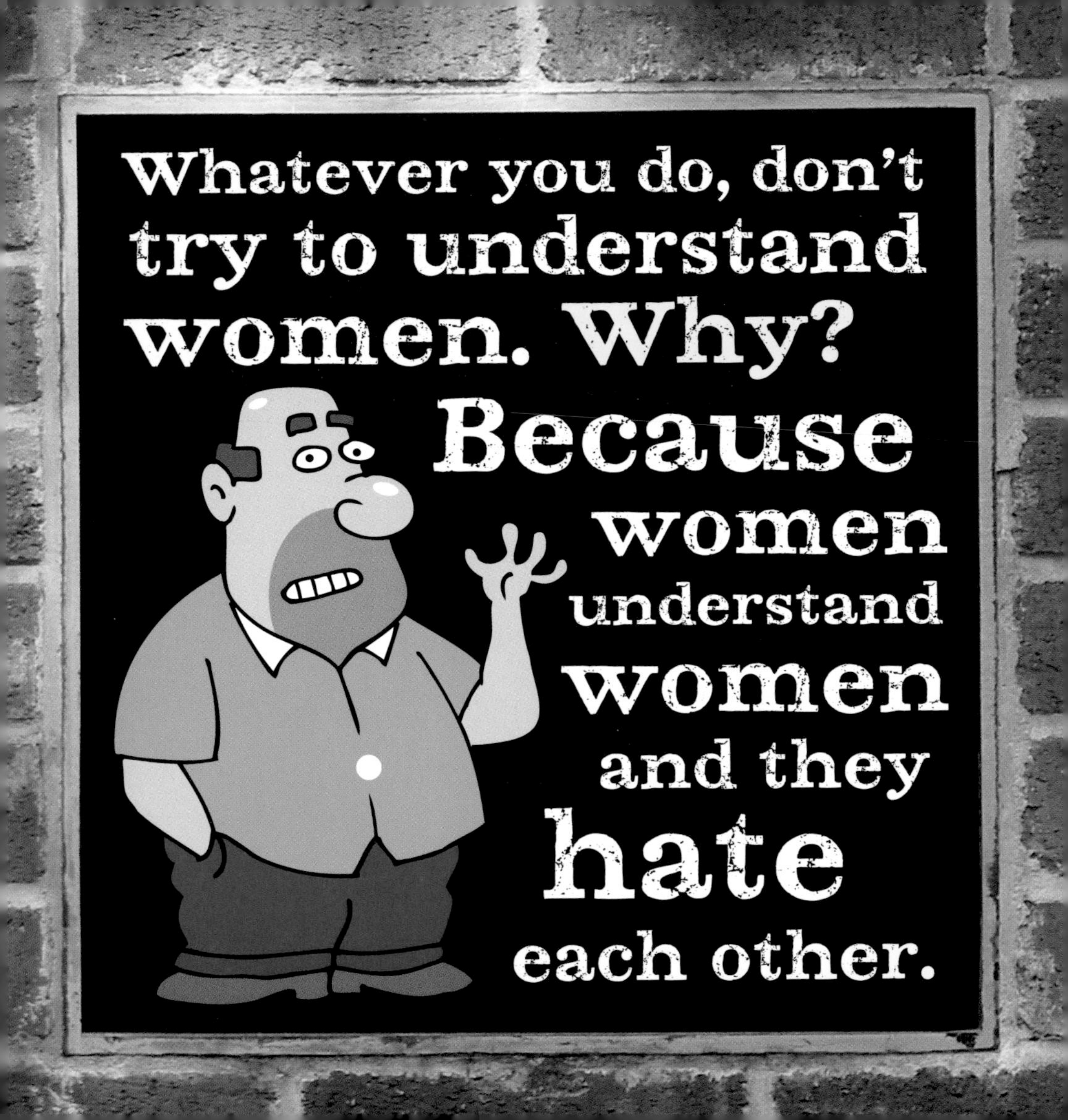
Whatever you do, don't try to understand women. Why?
Because women understand women and they hate each other.

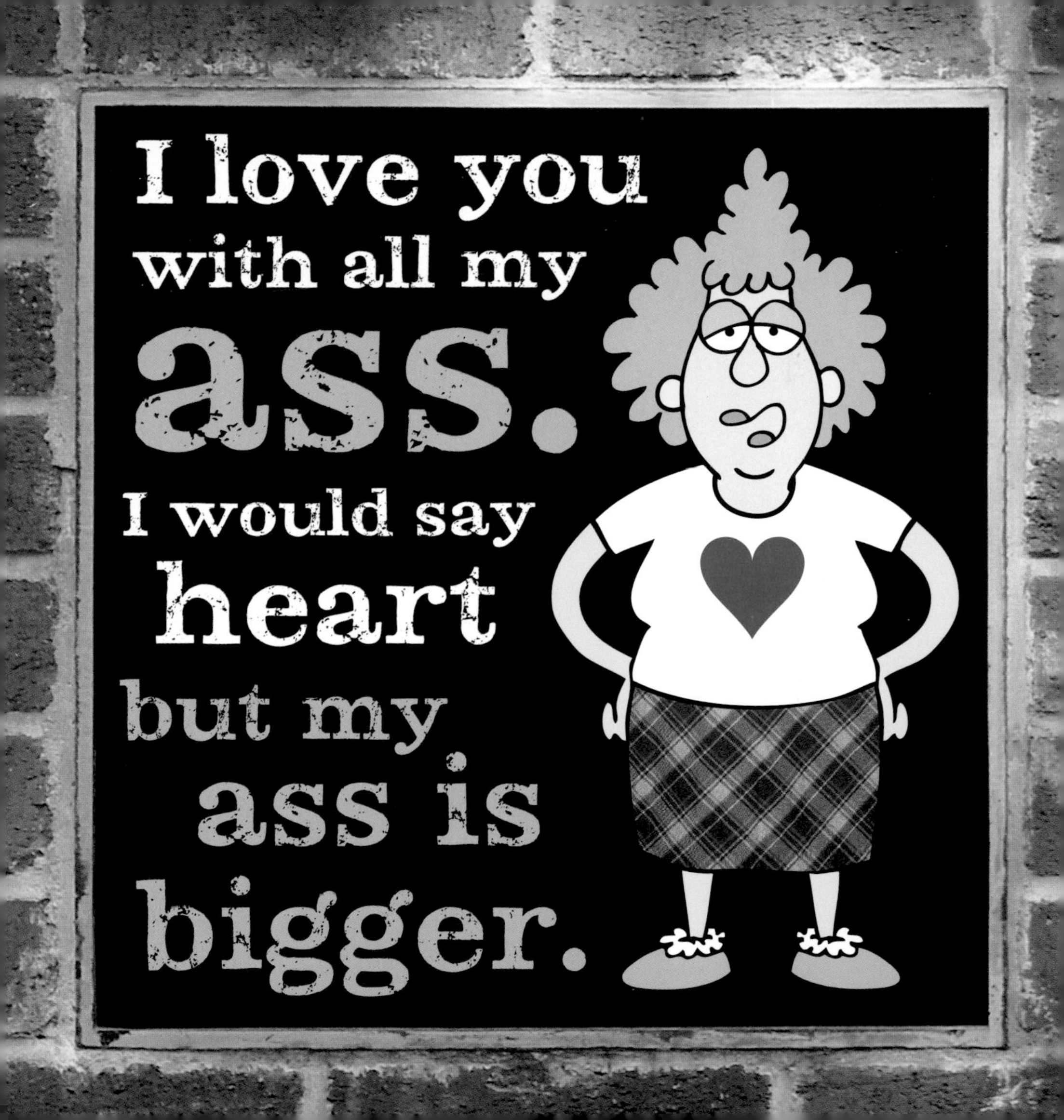
I love you
with all my
ass.
I would say
heart
but my
ass is
bigger.

Just once I'd like to see a pregnancy test commercial where the female is like, "Oh, crap!"

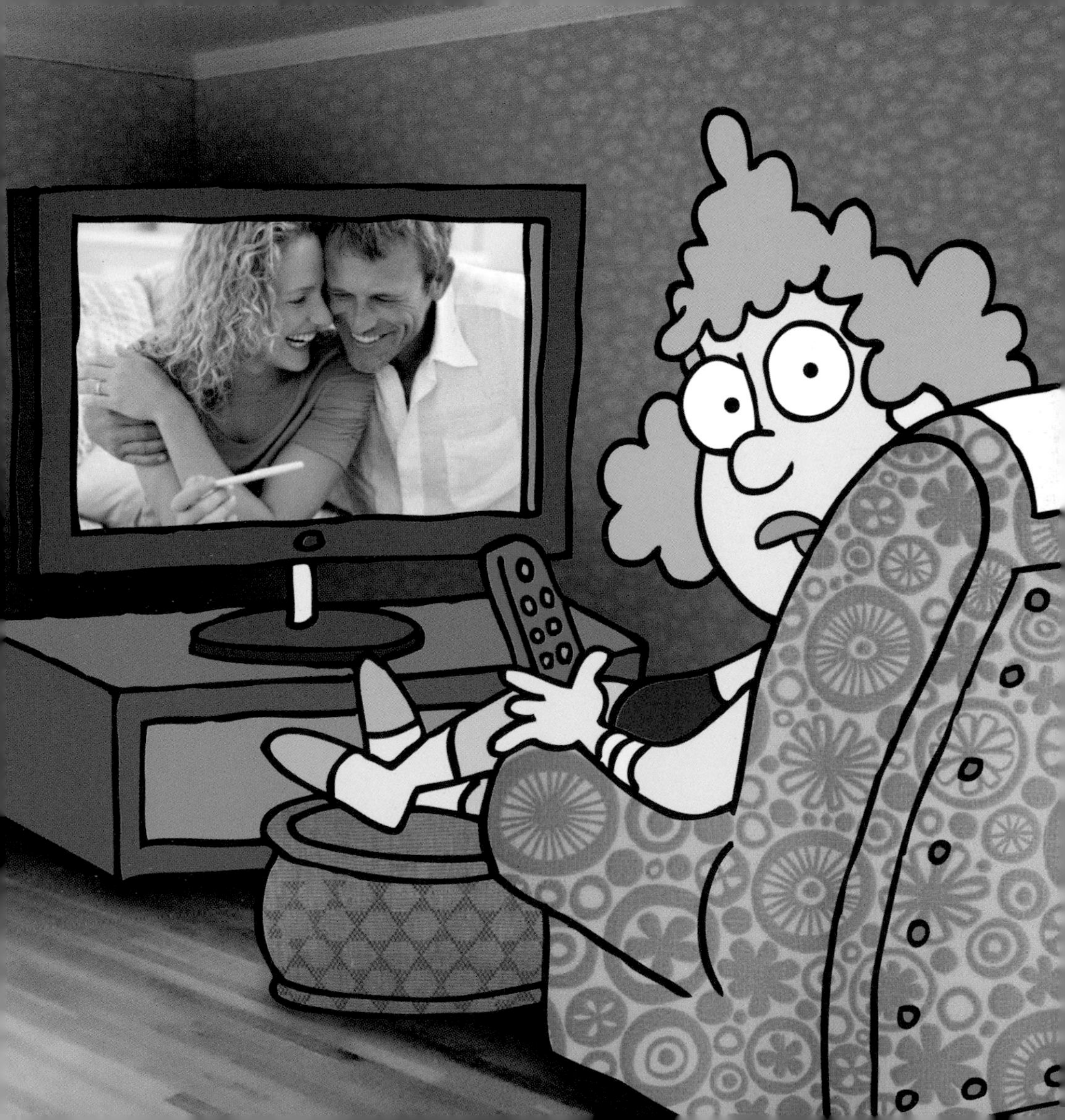

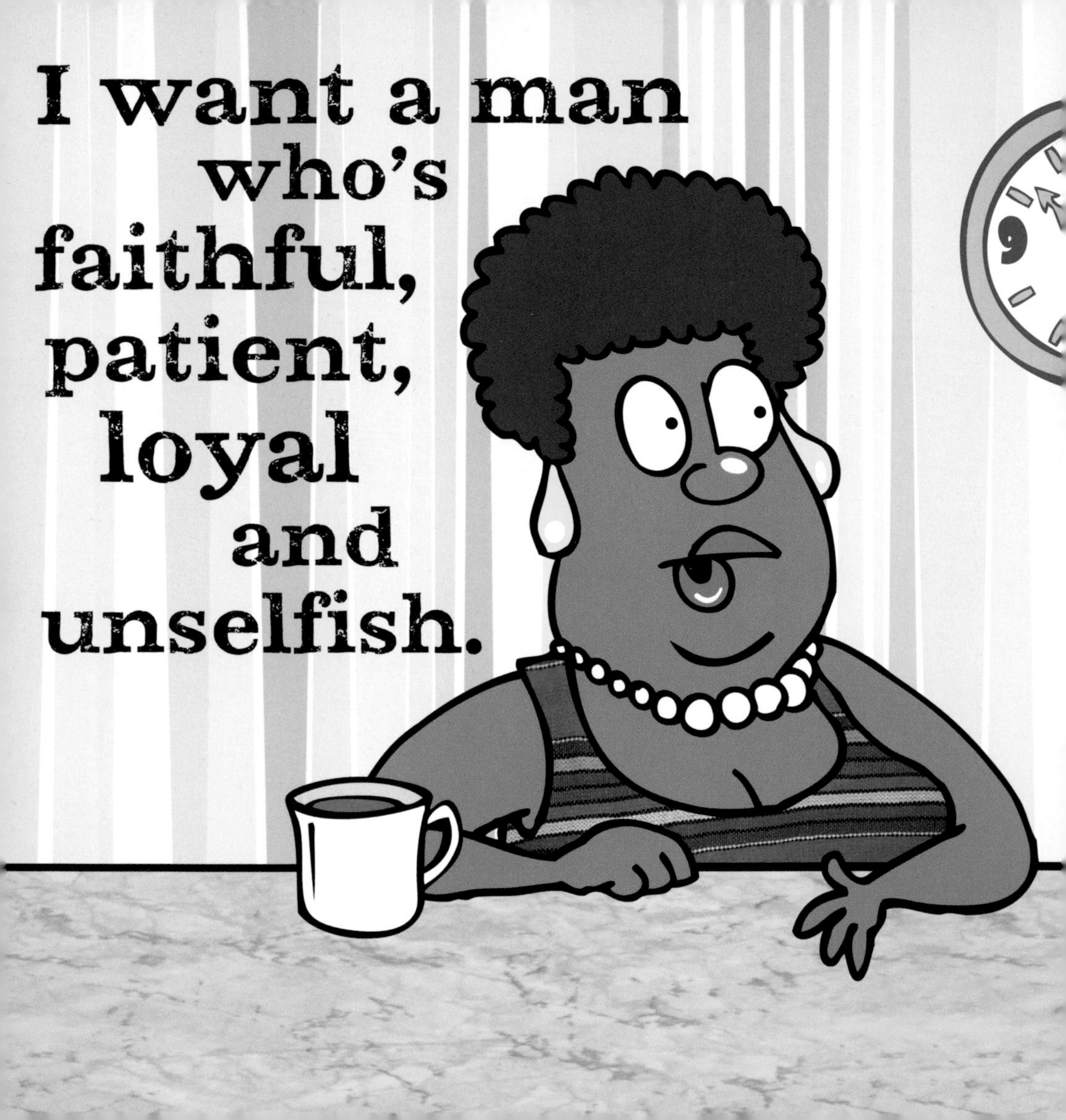
I want a man who's faithful, patient, loyal and unselfish.

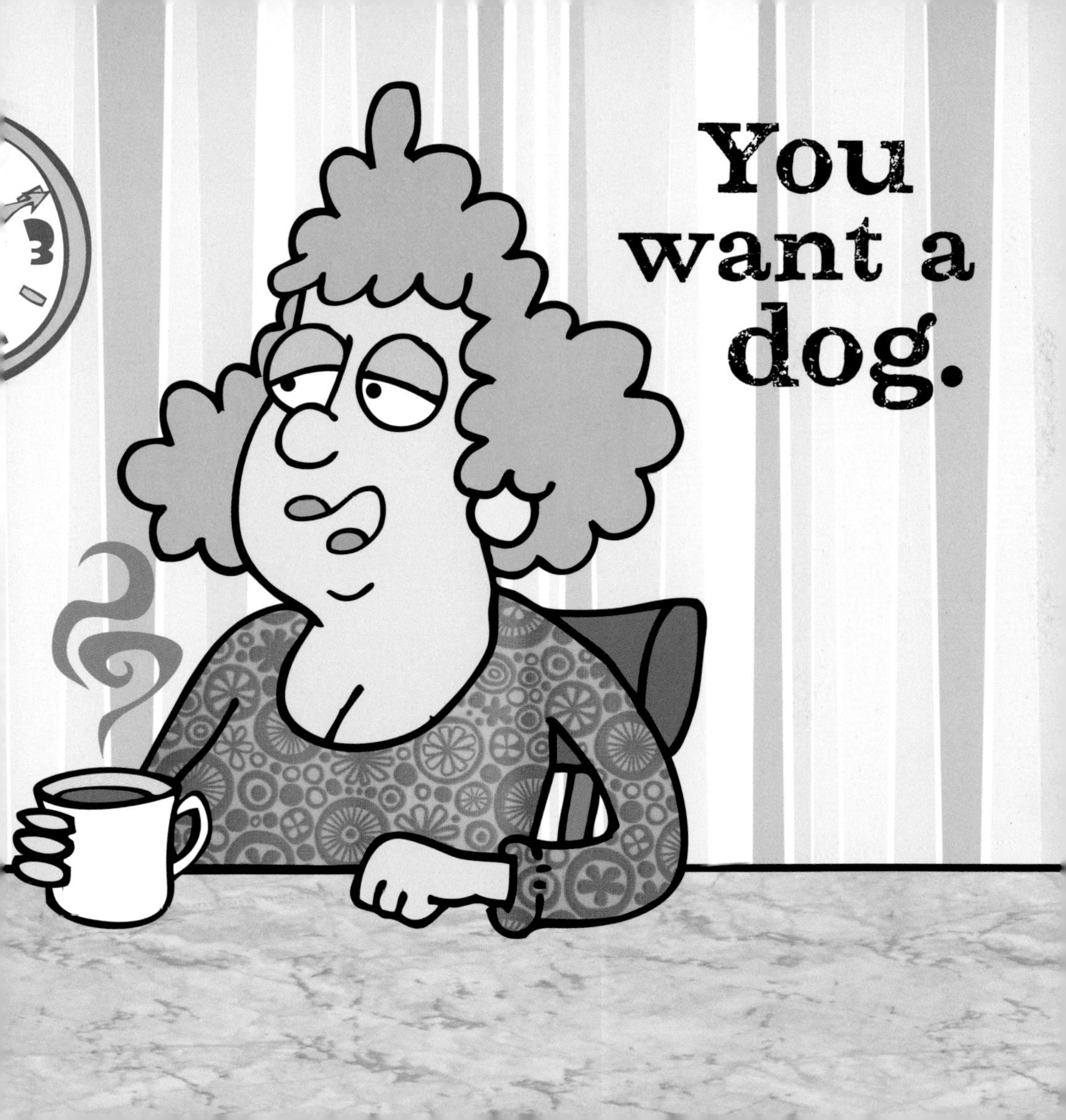
You want a dog.

I haven't spoken to my wife in years...

I don't want to interrupt her!

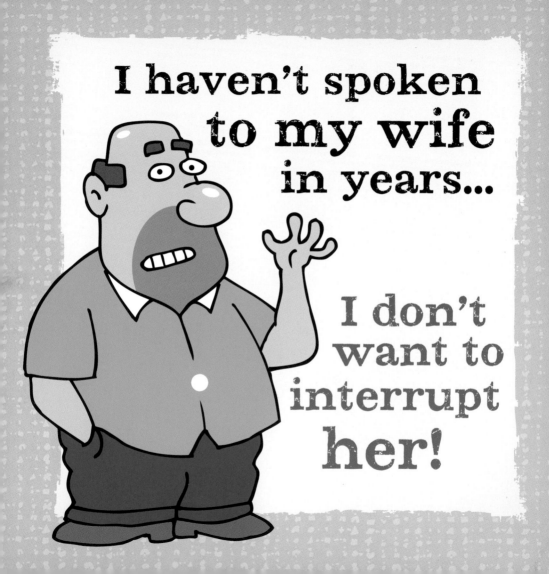

There are times I miss my first husband so badly.

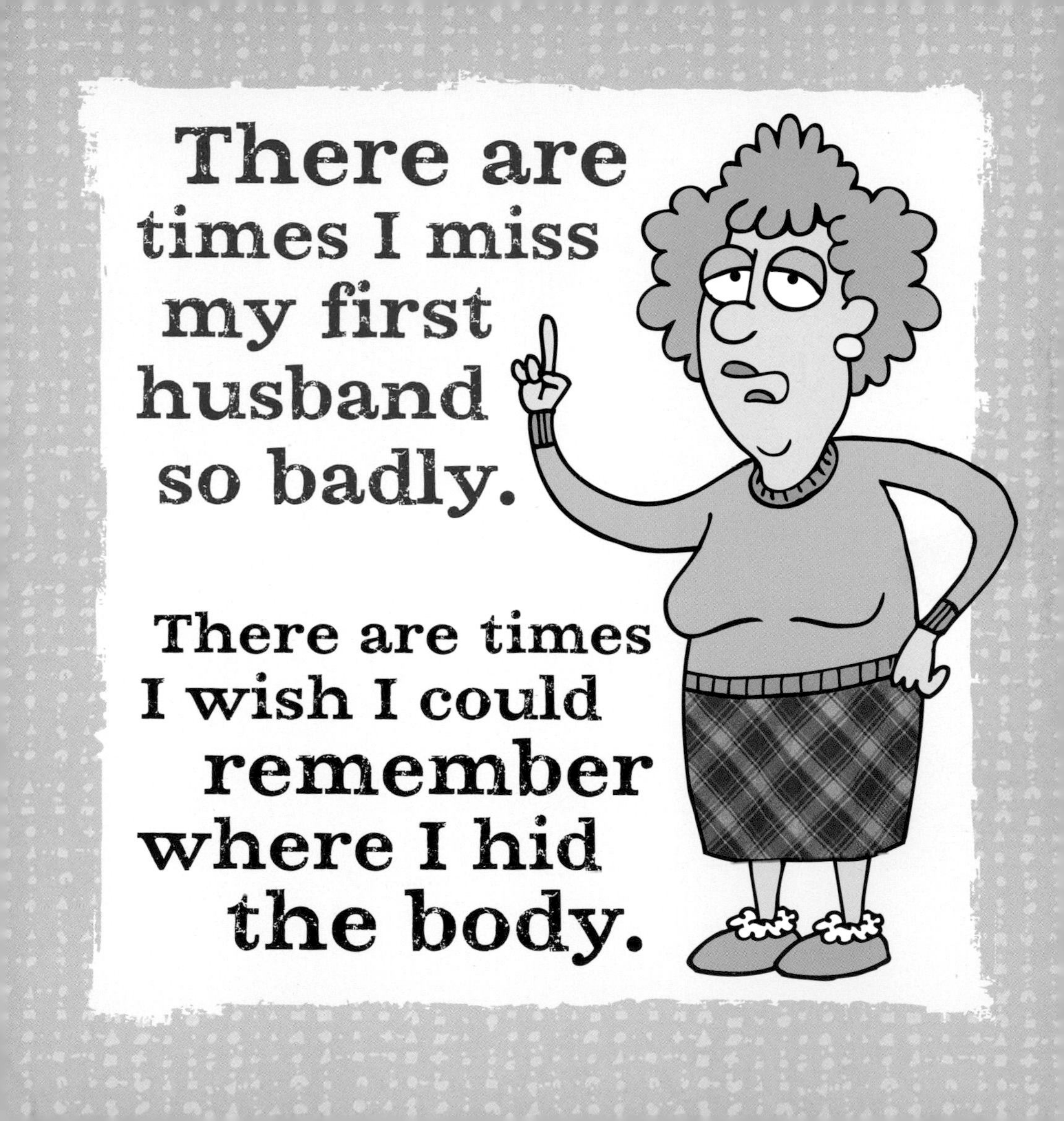

There are times I wish I could remember where I hid the body.

AUNTY ACID'S
RELATIONSHIP
ADVICE
No.15

Whatever happens, always make sure you're the crazy one.

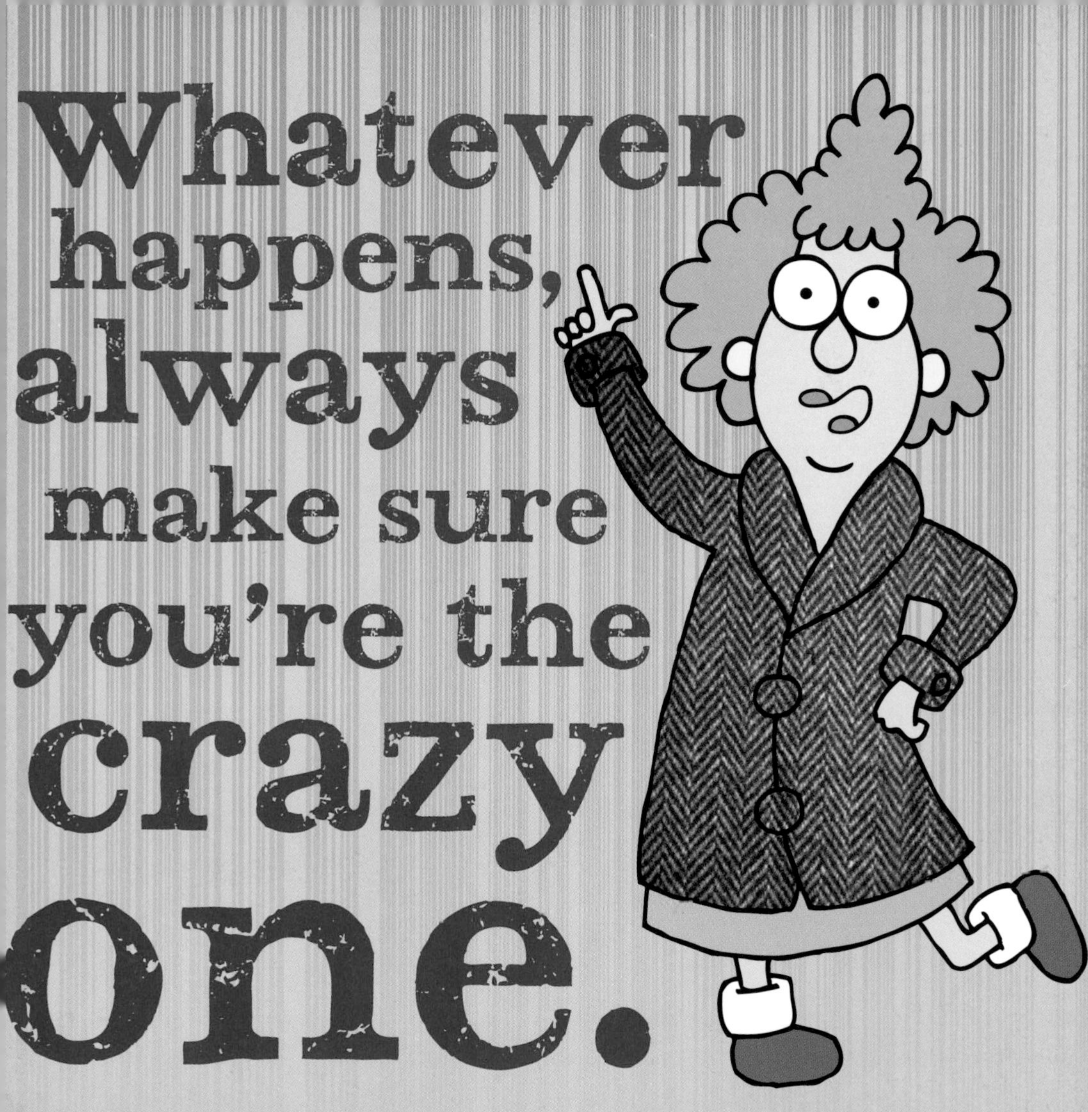

WISE WORDS ON TECHNOLOGY

Two things that really grind my gears are people and technology or, even worse, KIDS and technology. Putting your phone down and paying attention to those talking to you? There's an app for that—it's called respect!

Sure in my day we had our own type of social networking, it was called "go outside and play."

I was thinking, if you had to pedal to power up the computer, you'd be a real Skinny Minnie in no time!

So put your phone down for a second, log off and enjoy my take on texting, tweeting and all things technological—now try saying that without your teeth in.

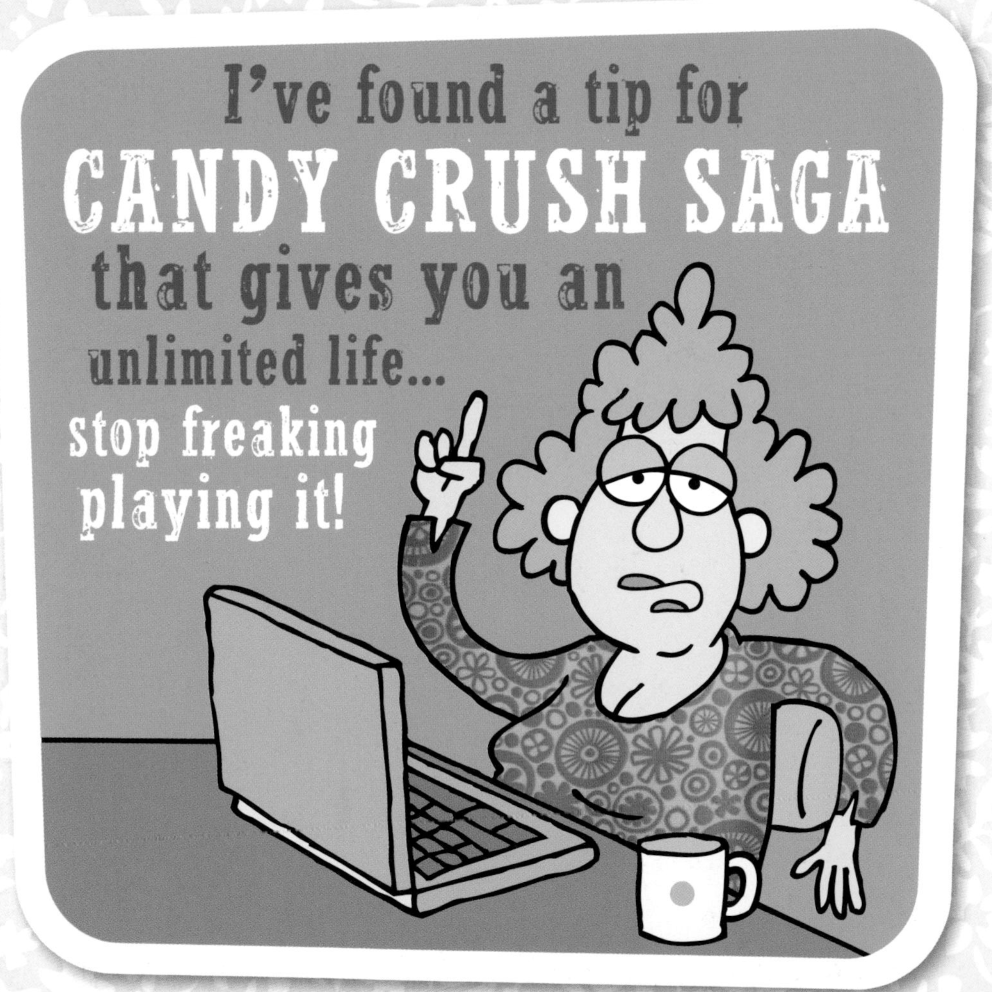
I've found a tip for
CANDY CRUSH SAGA
that gives you an
unlimited life...
stop freaking
playing it!

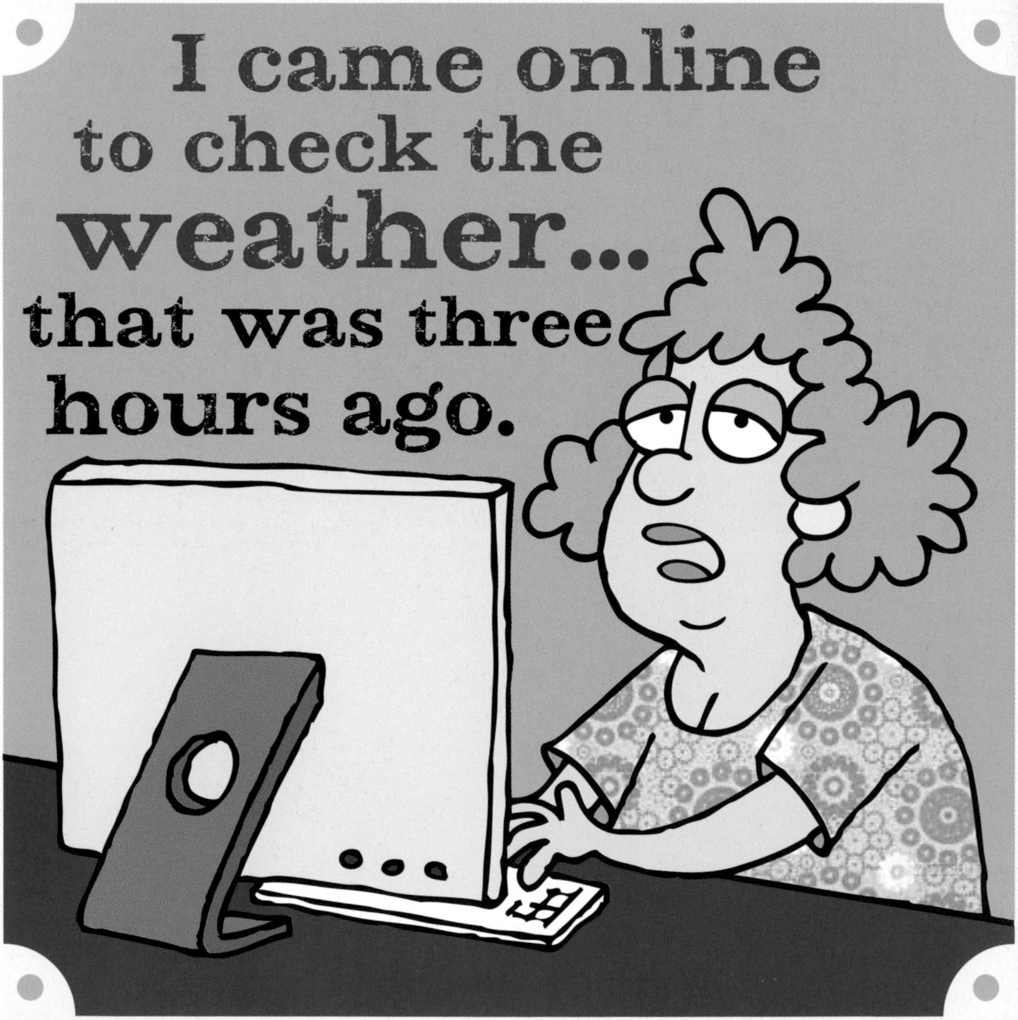
I came online
to check the
weather...
that was three
hours ago.

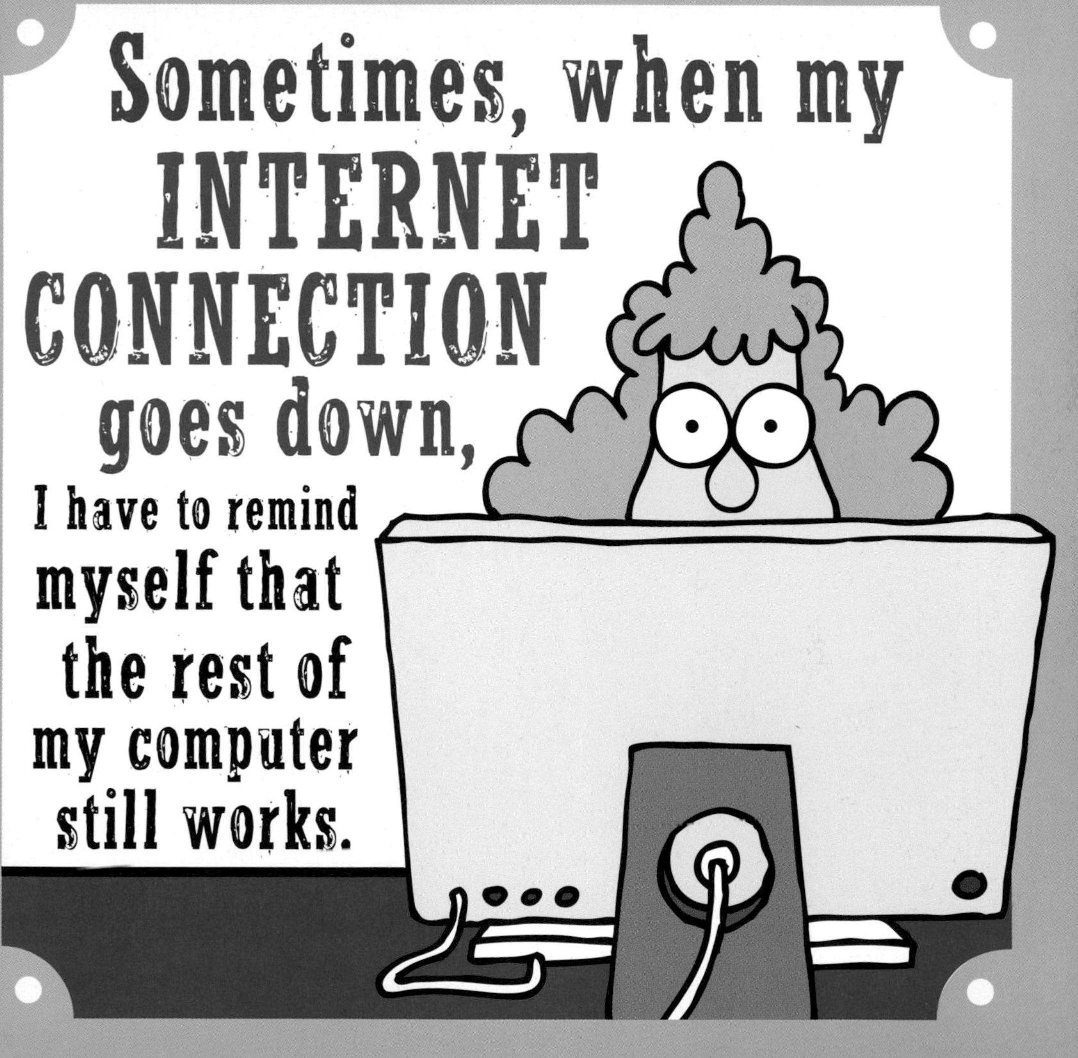
Sometimes, when my
INTERNET
CONNECTION
goes down,
I have to remind
myself that
the rest of
my computer
still works.

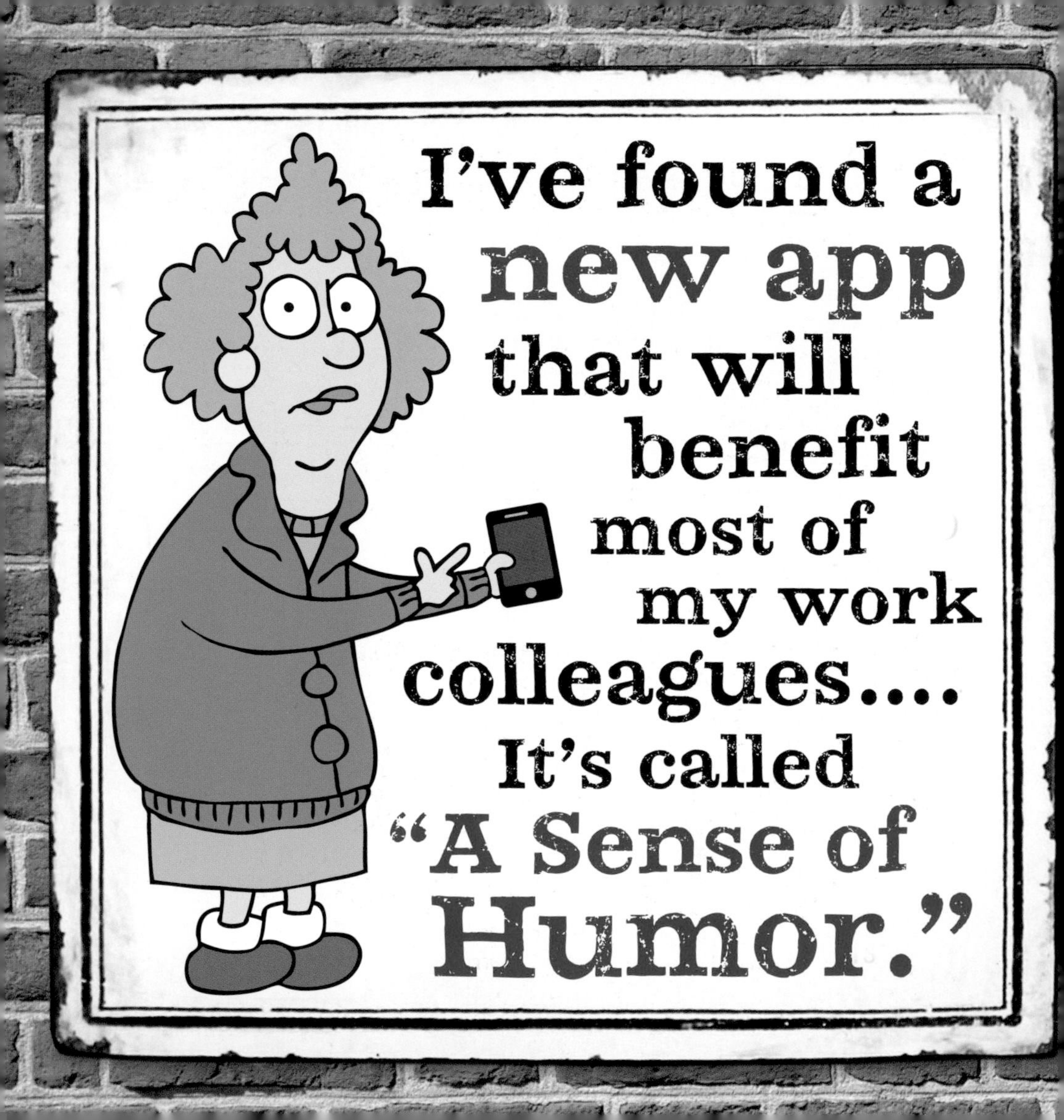
I've found a new app that will benefit most of my work colleagues.... It's called "A Sense of Humor."

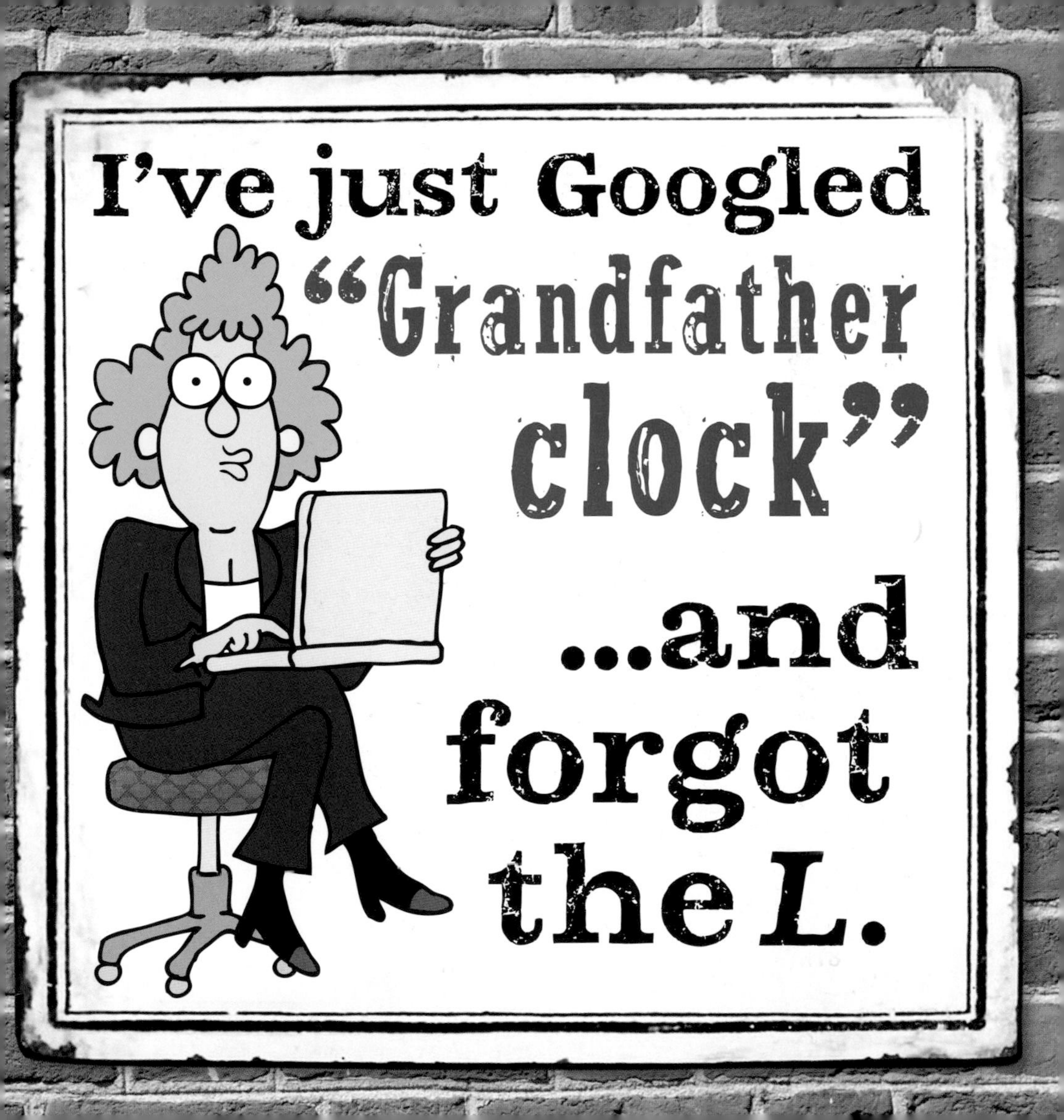
I've just Googled
"Grandfather
clock"
...and
forgot
the L.

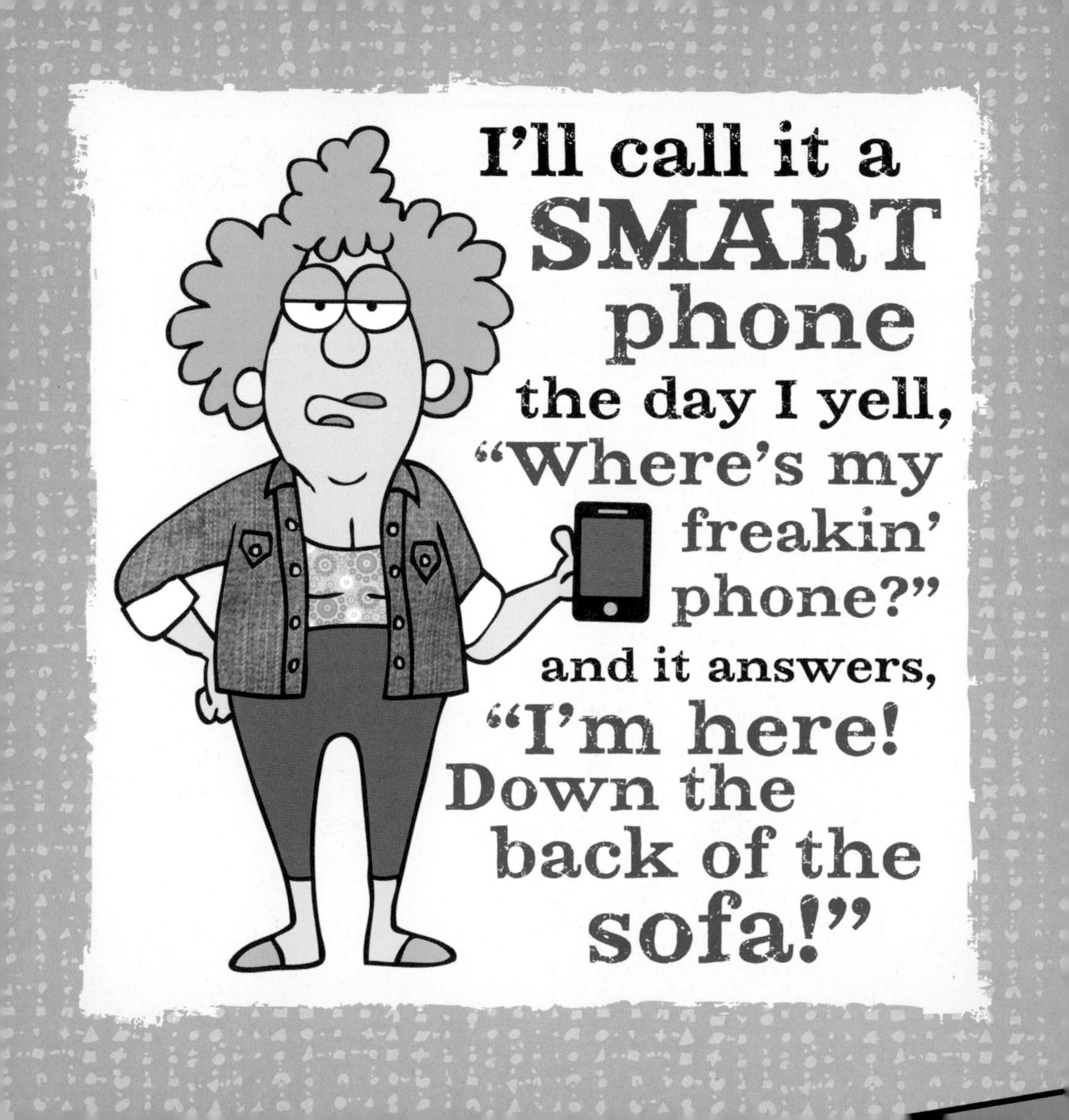

I'll call it a
SMART
phone
the day I yell,
"Where's my
freakin'
phone?"
and it answers,
"I'm here!
Down the
back of the
sofa!"

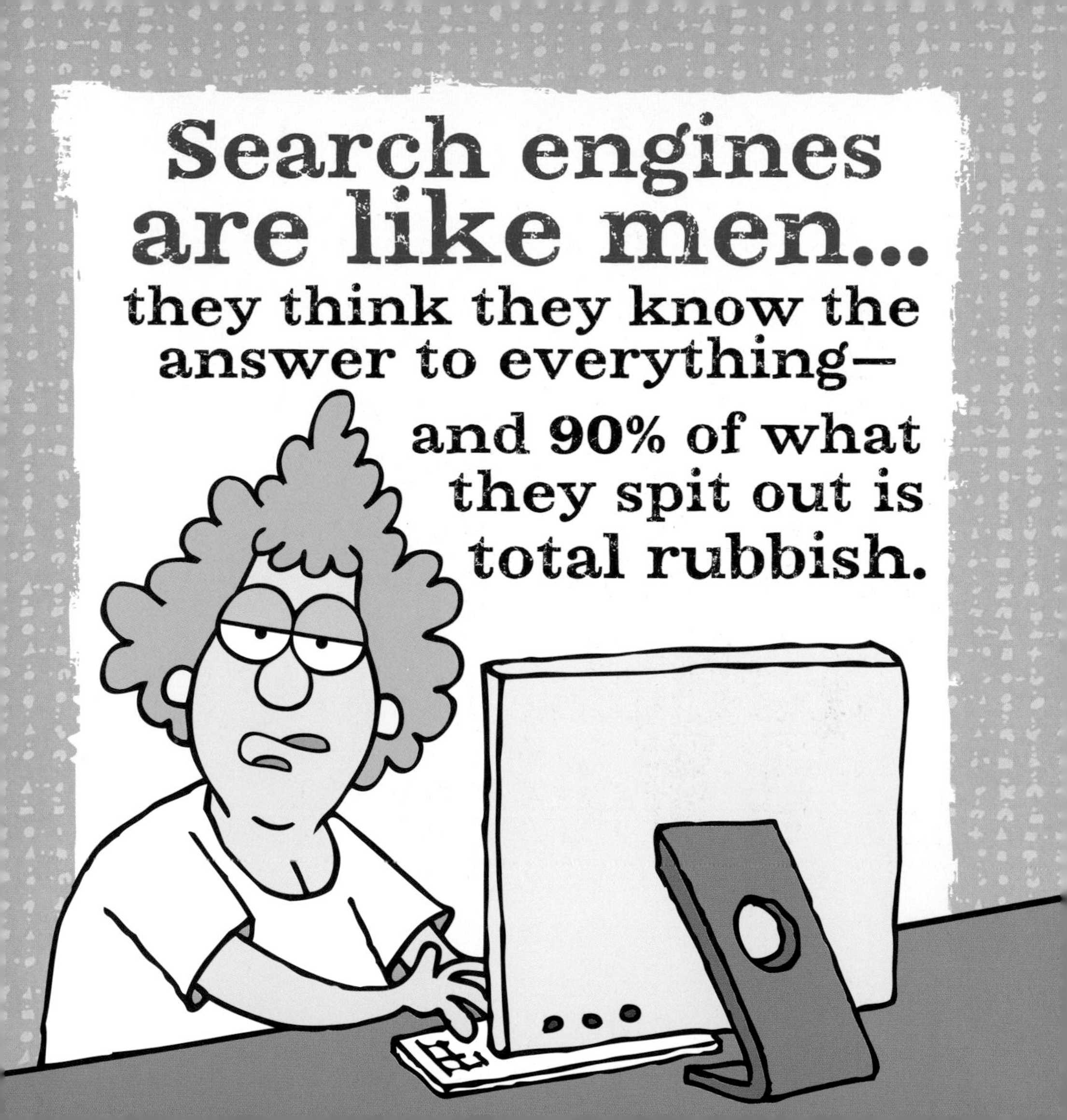
Search engines are like men...
they think they know the answer to everything—
and 90% of what they spit out is total rubbish.

I told my friend there was actually a life beyond the Internet and she should check it out sometime...

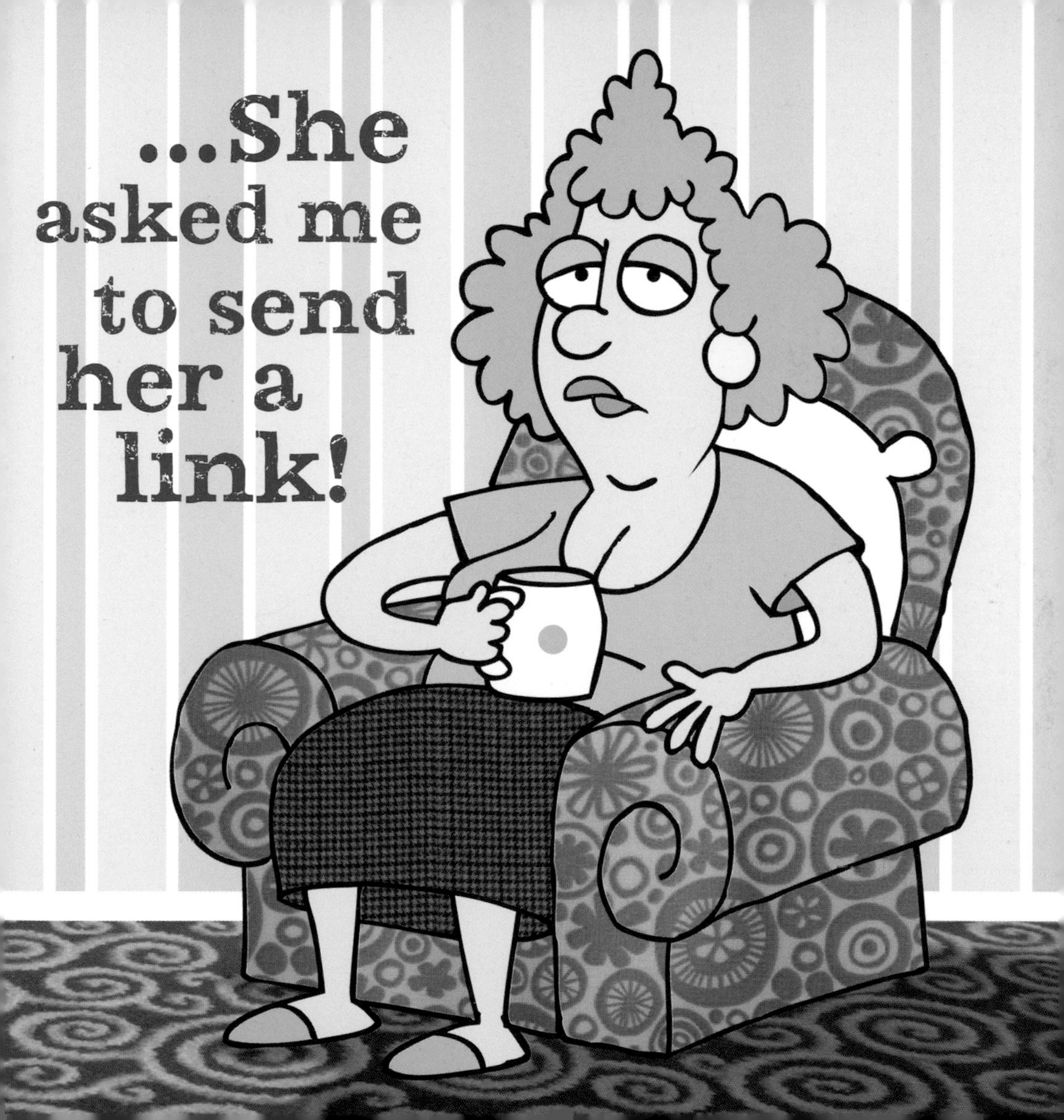
...She
asked me
to send
her a
link!

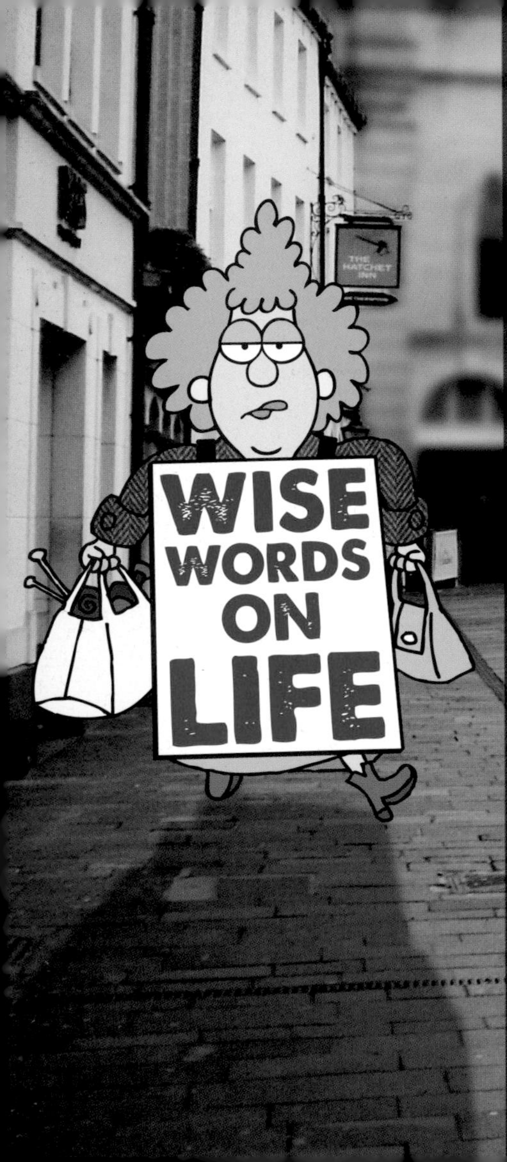
WISE
WORDS
ON
LIFE

Life is short, so I say smile while you still have teeth. Saying that, if good things are meant to be in store for me, where is this freakin' store? I'd like a word with the manager.

Of course, during the tough times, I've felt like throwing in the towel, but then I remember that just means more laundry for me!

The secret key to lifelong happiness is easy—stay away from a**holes.

Sometimes I'm not sure if life is just passing me by or trying to run me over. But what I do know is, I'm here for a good time, not a long time. So I've gathered you up some more wisdom over the following pages. Read, learn and enjoy.

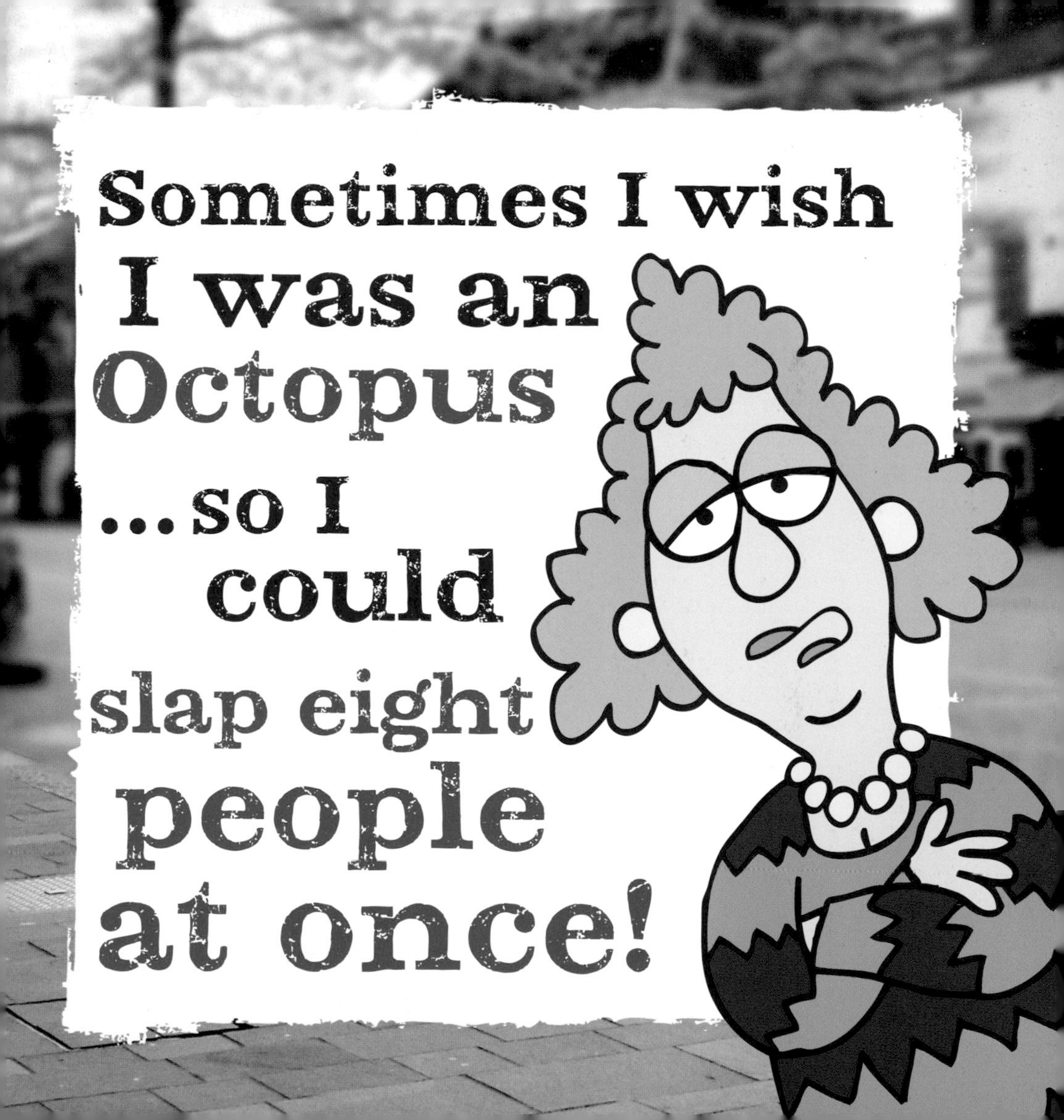
Sometimes I wish
I was an
Octopus
...so I
could
slap eight
people
at once!

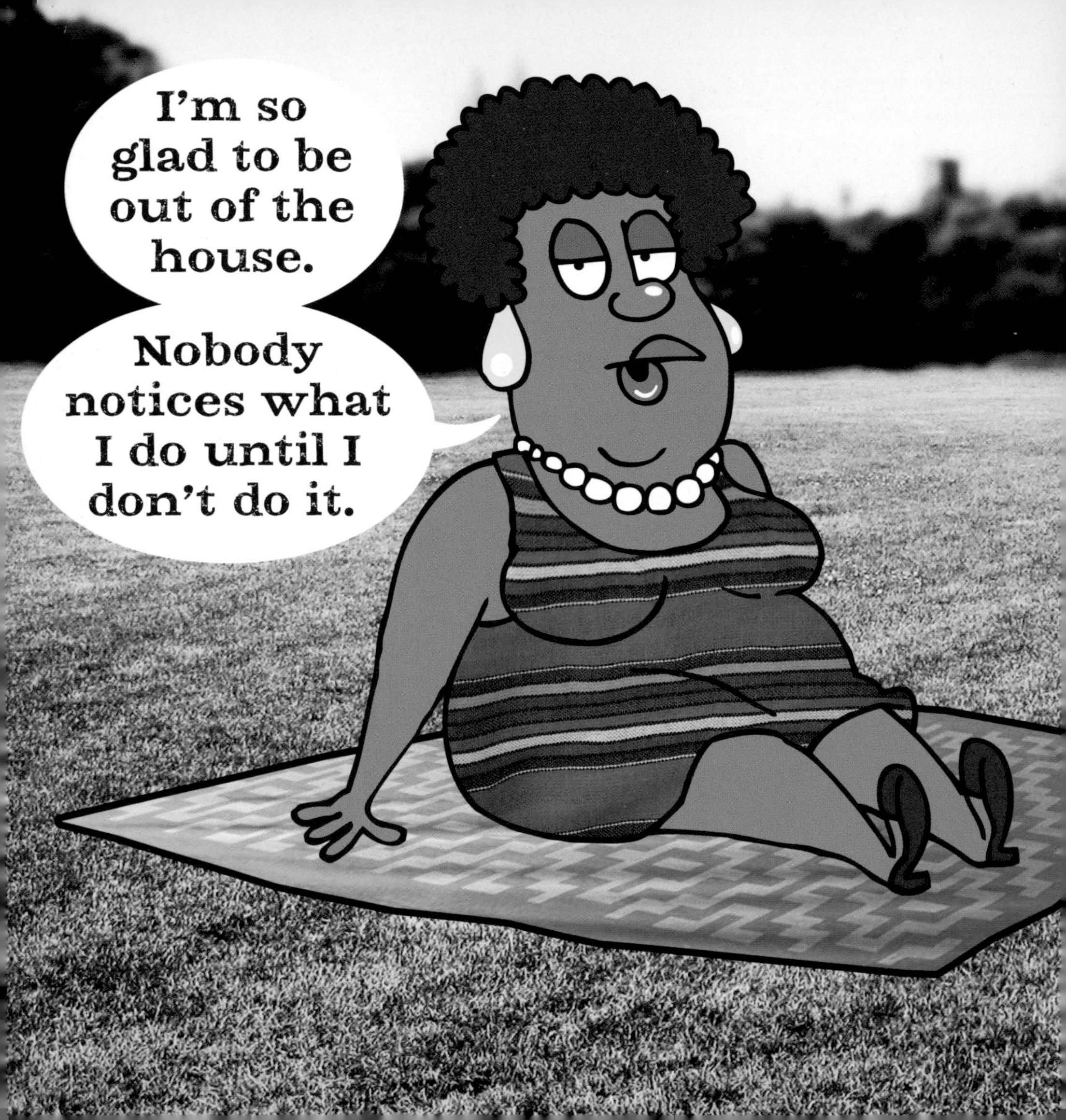
I'm so glad to be out of the house.
Nobody notices what I do until I don't do it.

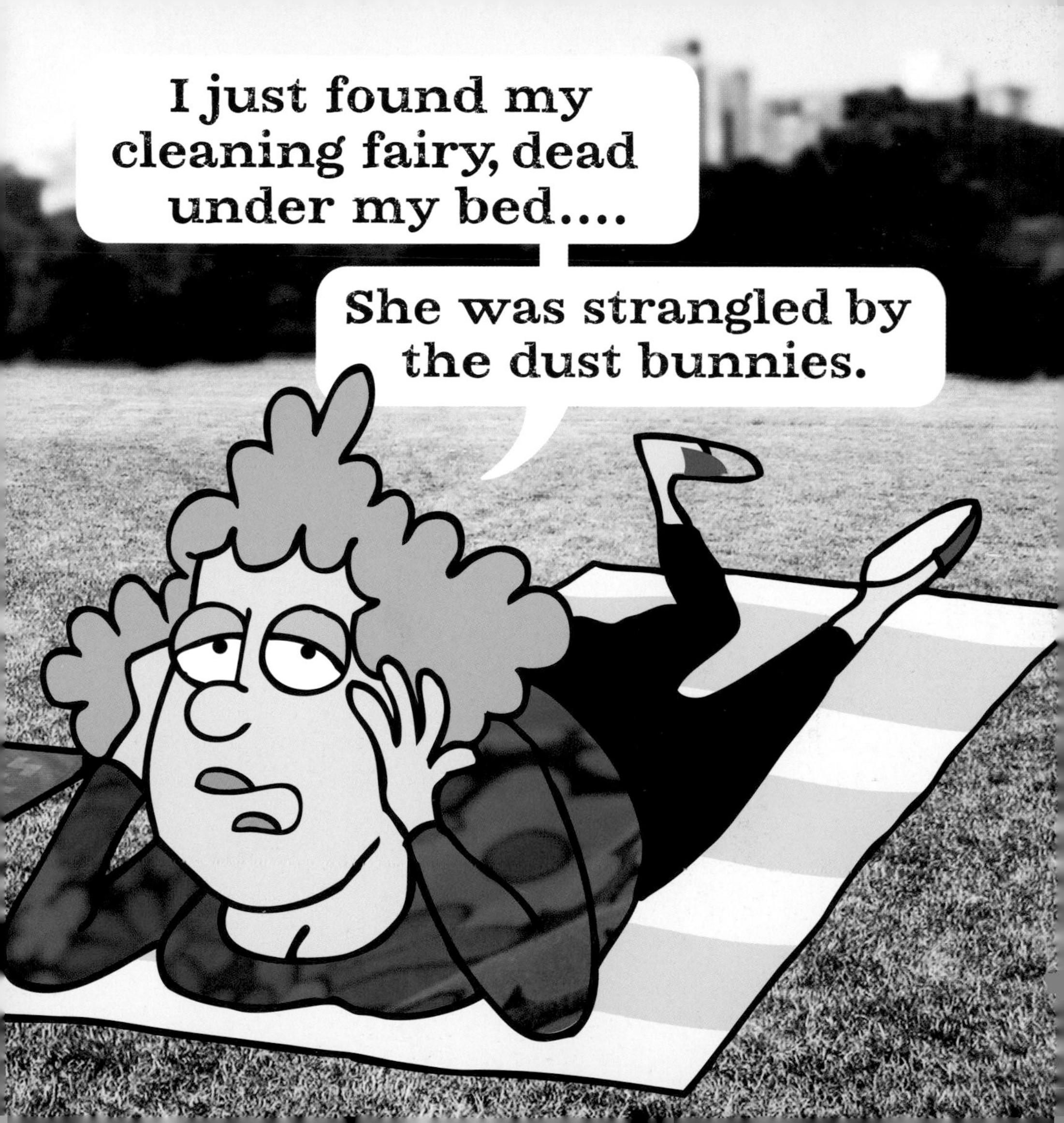
I just found my cleaning fairy, dead under my bed....
She was strangled by the dust bunnies.

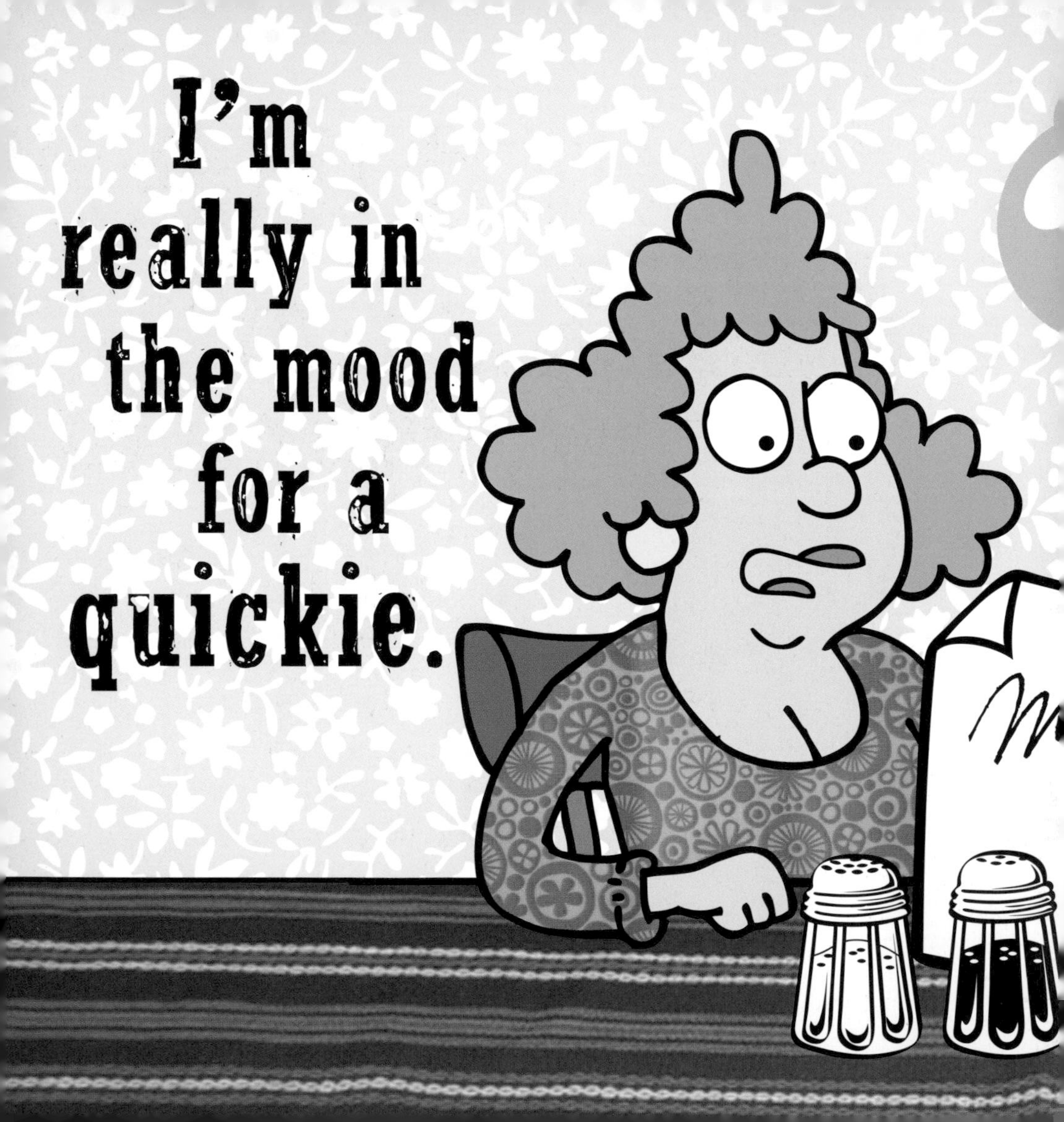
I'm really in the mood for a quickie.

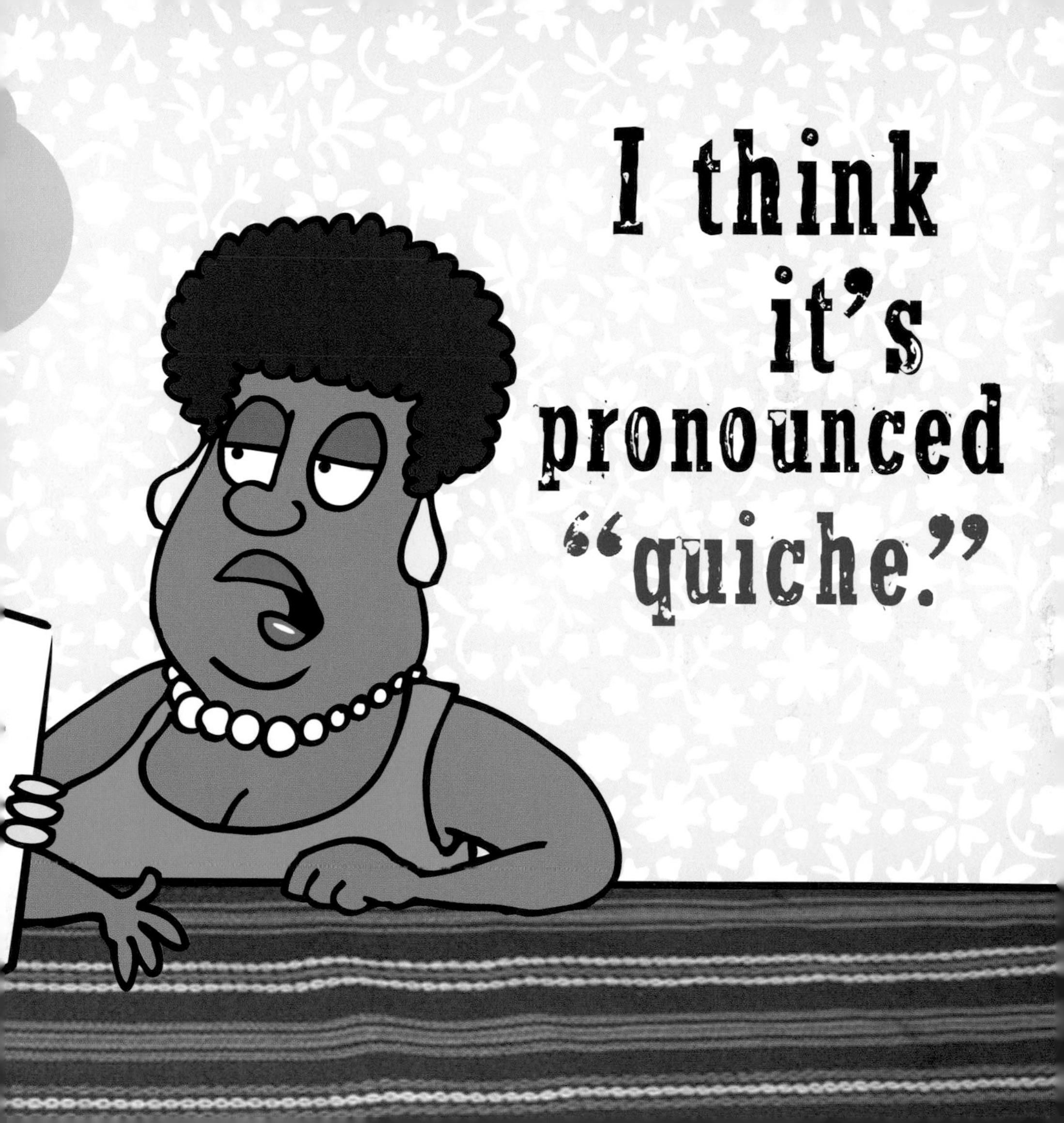
I think it's pronounced "quiche."

When I get naked in the bathroom, the shower gets turned on.

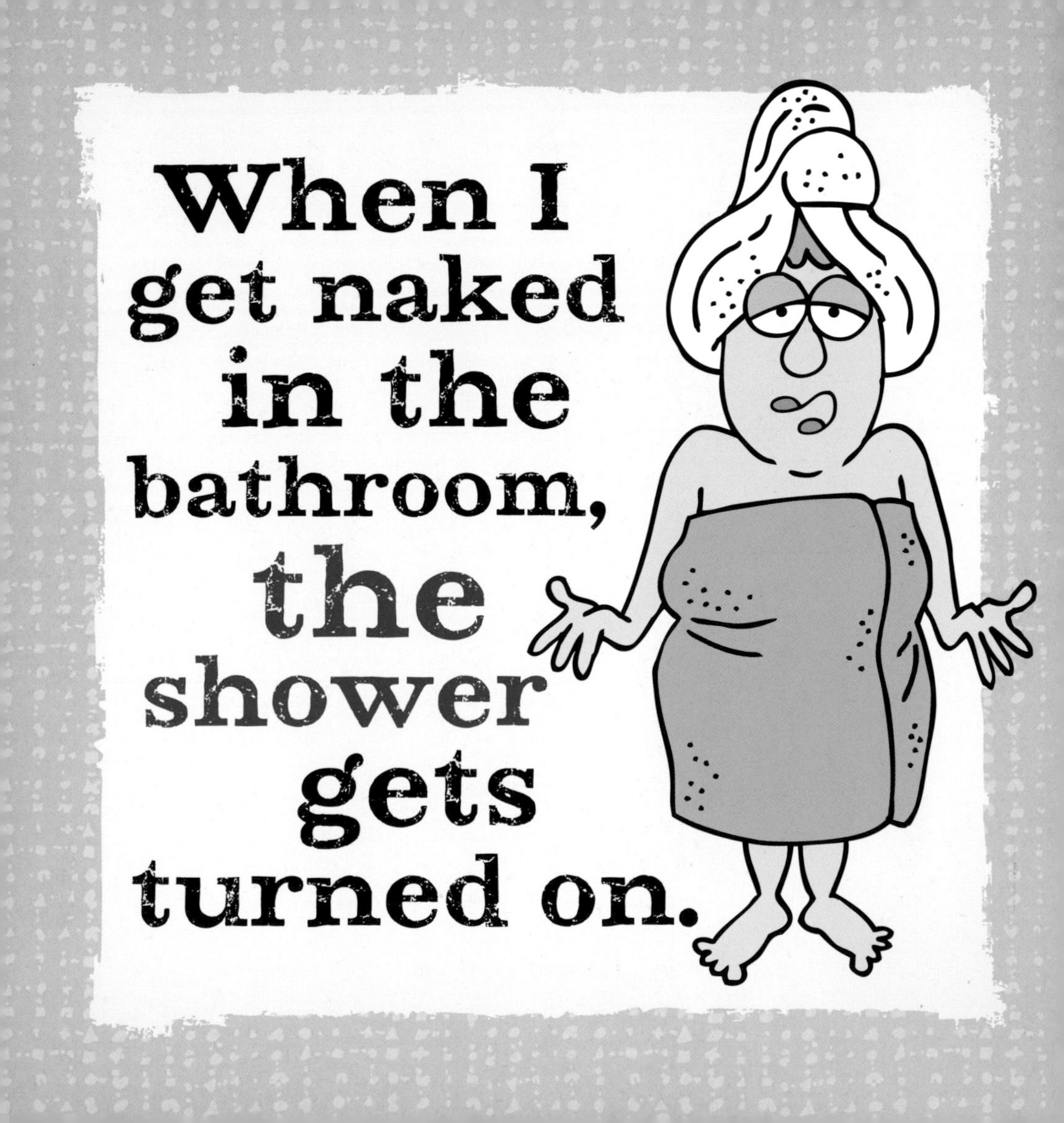

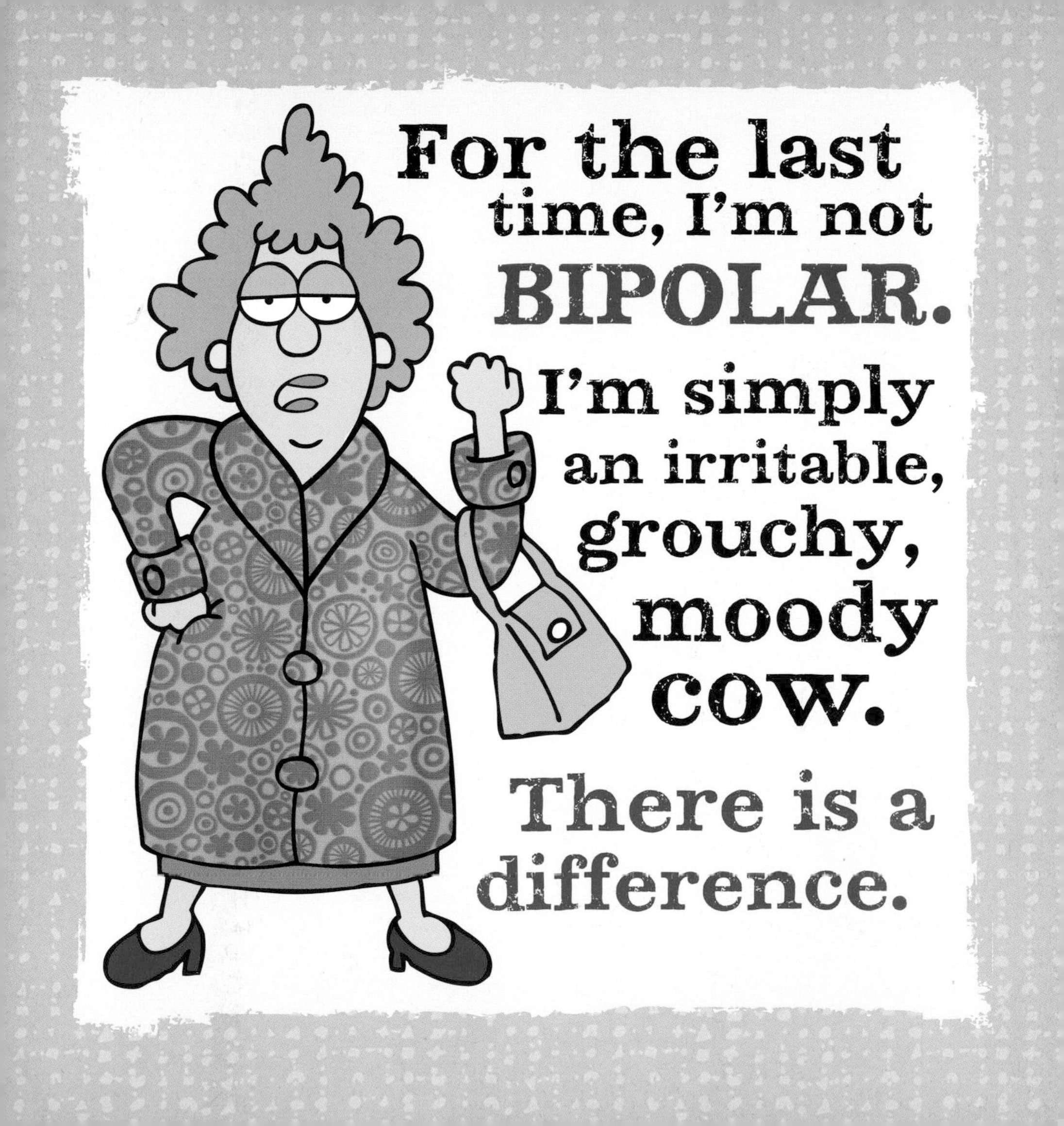

For the last time, I'm not BIPOLAR.

I'm simply an irritable, grouchy, moody cow.

There is a difference.

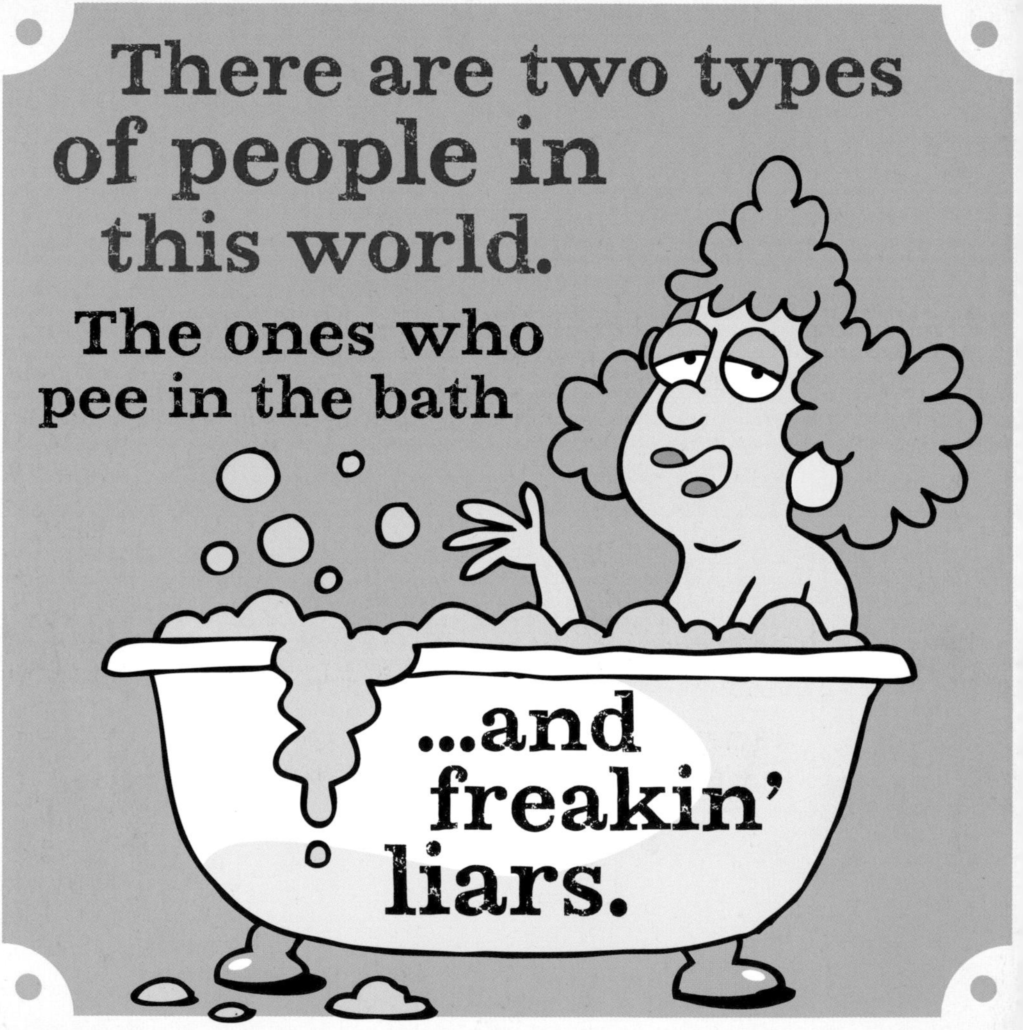
There are two types of people in this world.
The ones who pee in the bath
...and freakin' liars.

20 years ago we had Johnny Cash, Bob Hope and Steve Jobs.

Now we have NO CASH, NO HOPE and NO JOBS.

Please don't let Kevin BACON die!

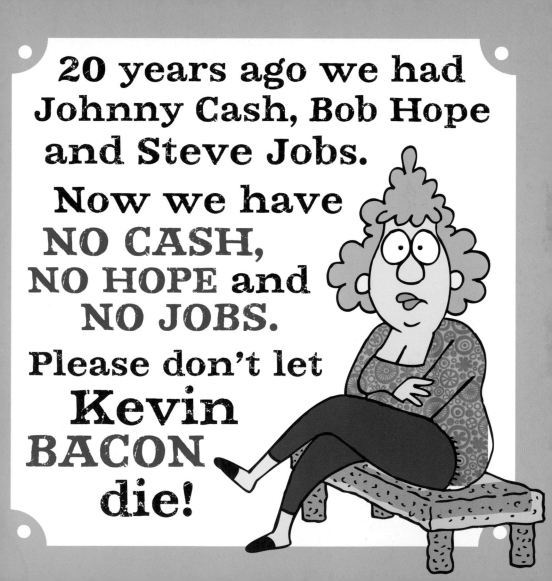

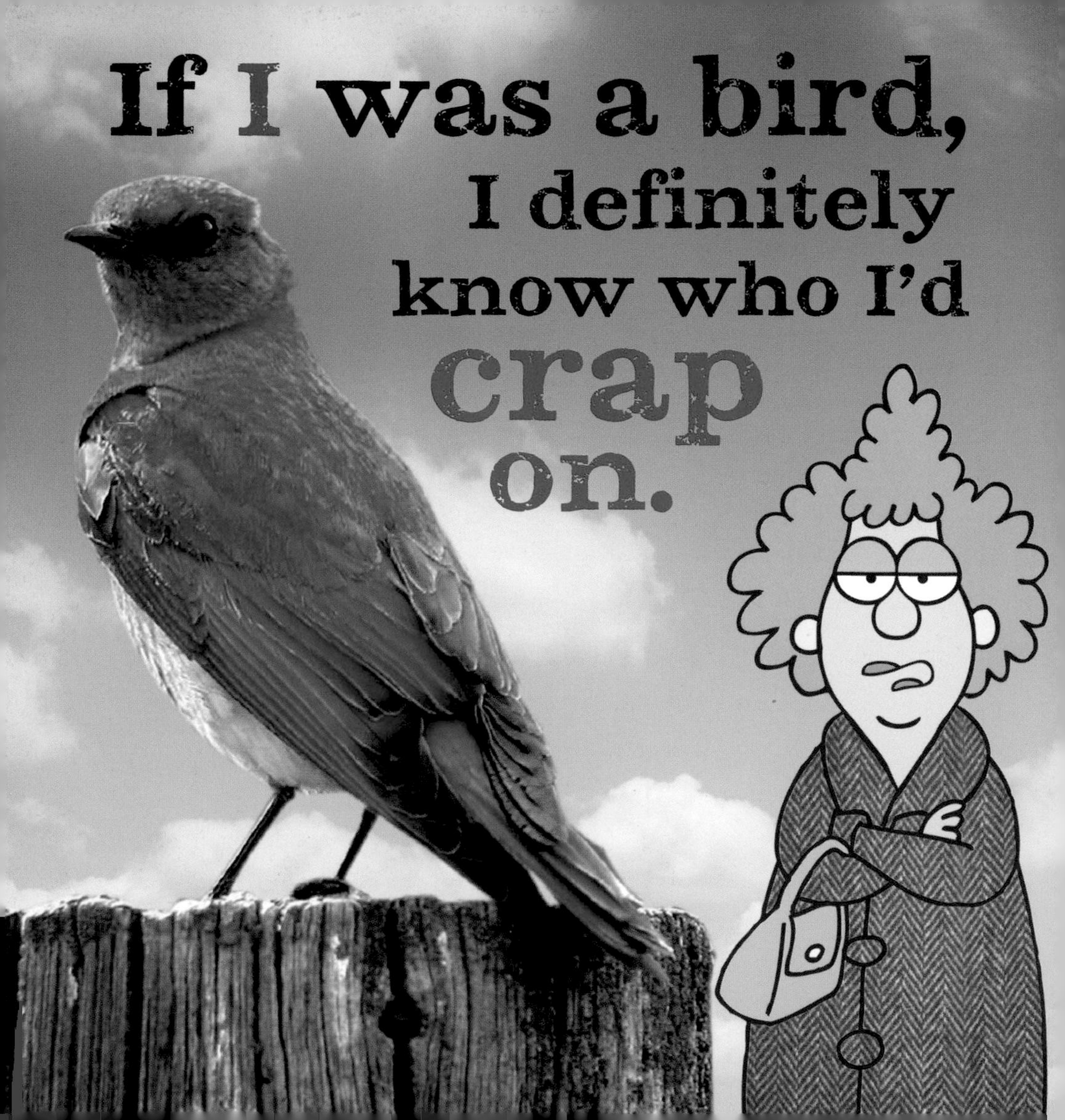
If I was a bird,
I definitely
know who I'd
crap
on.

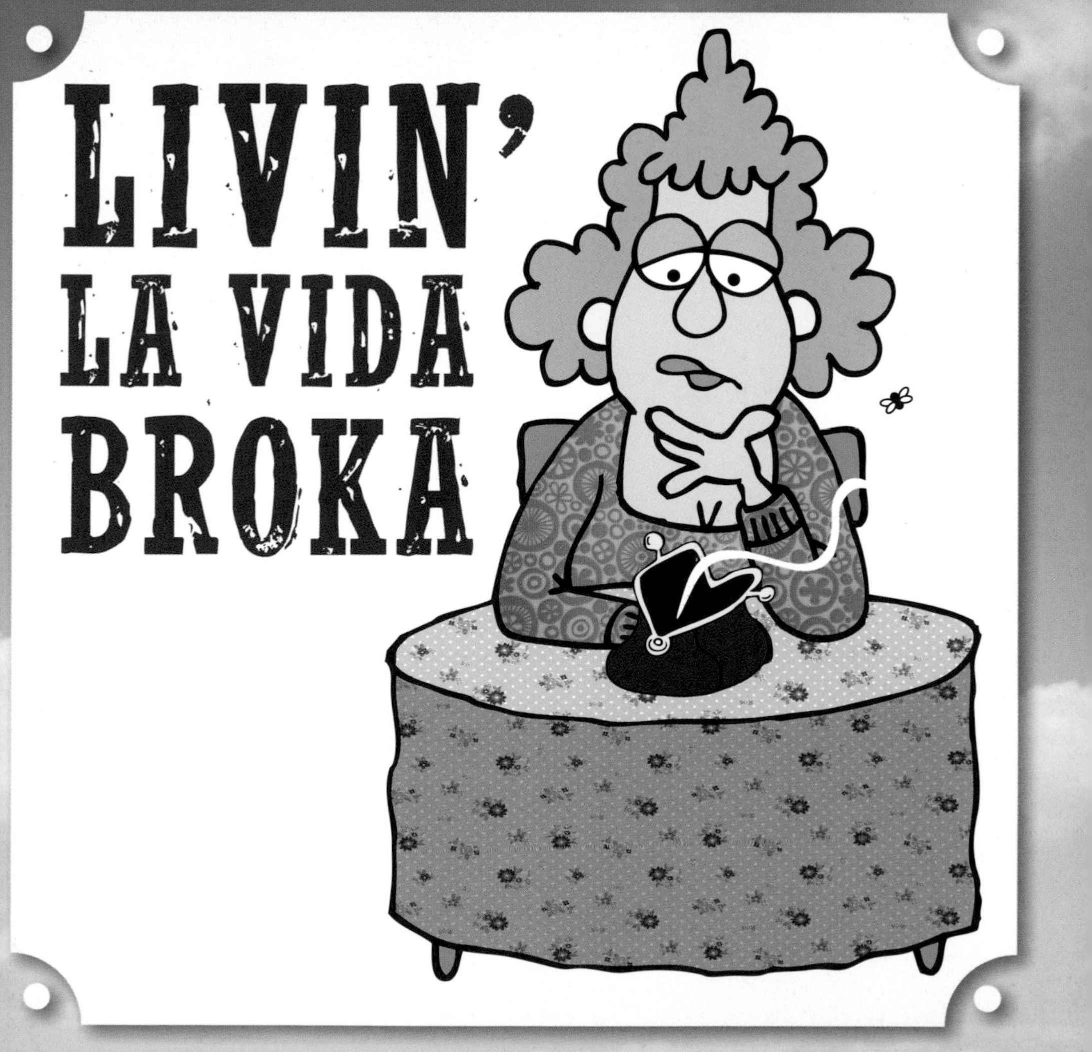
LIVIN'
LA VIDA
BROKA

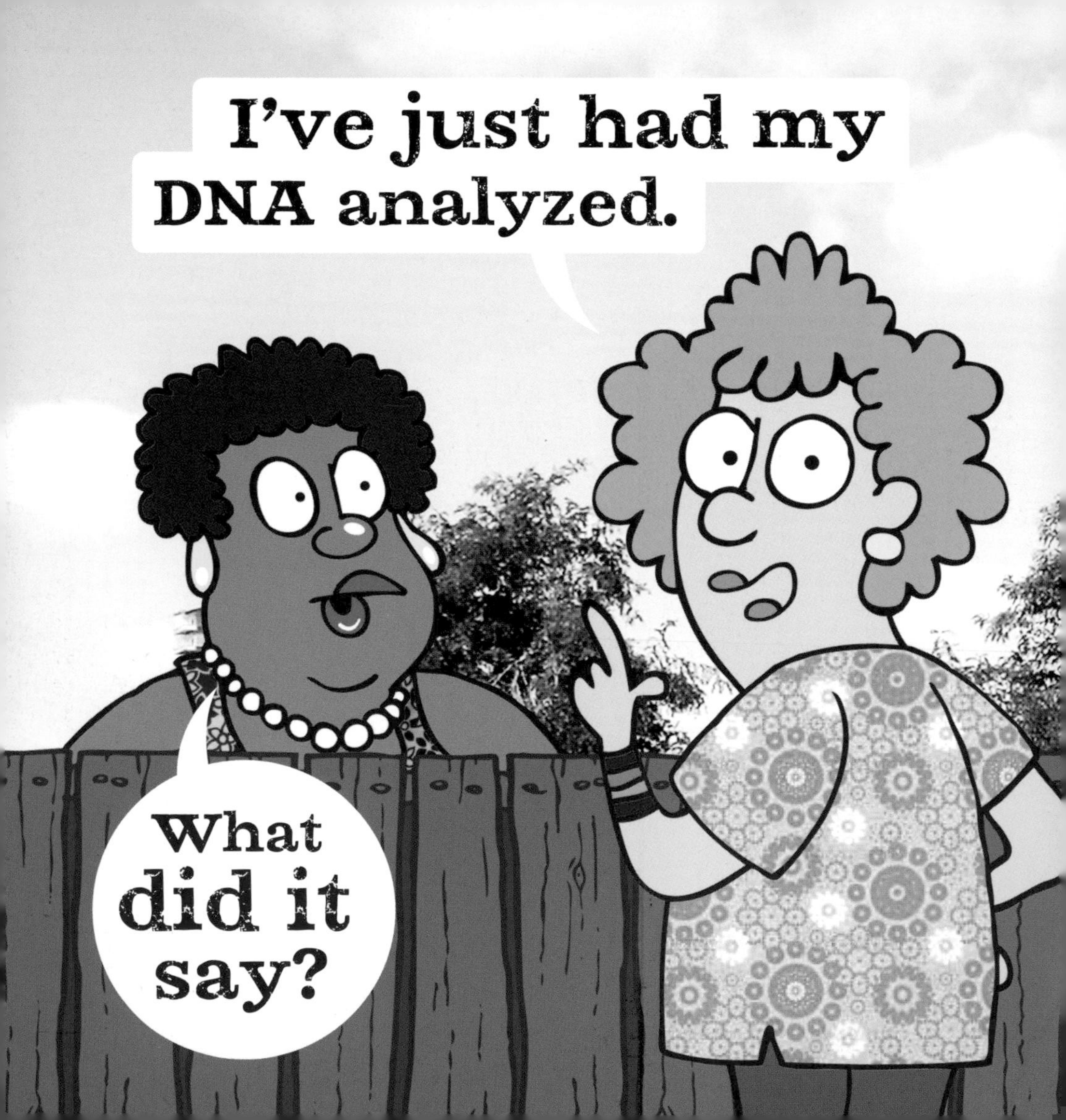
I've just had my DNA analyzed.
What did it say?

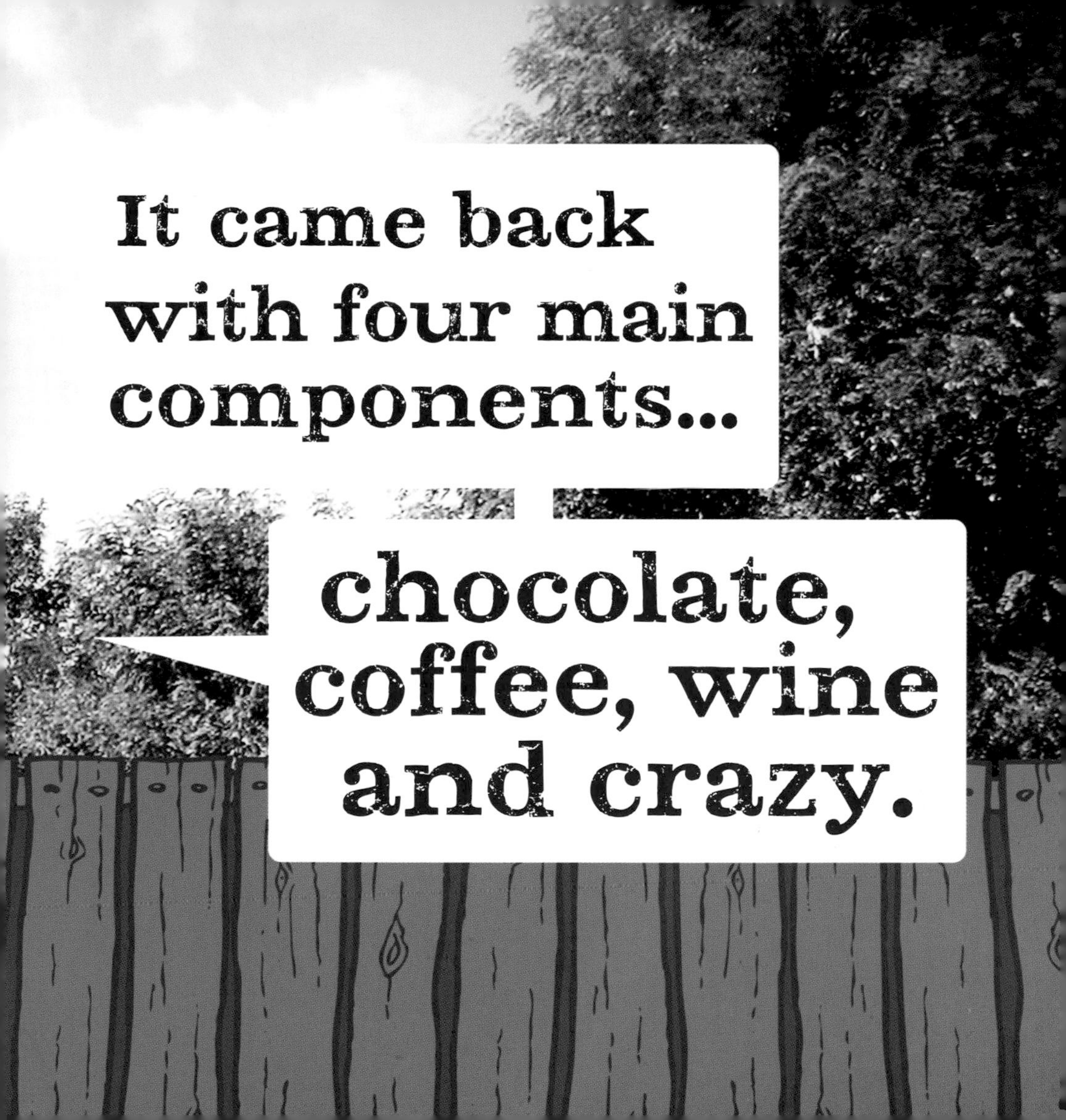
It came back with four main components...
chocolate, coffee, wine and crazy.

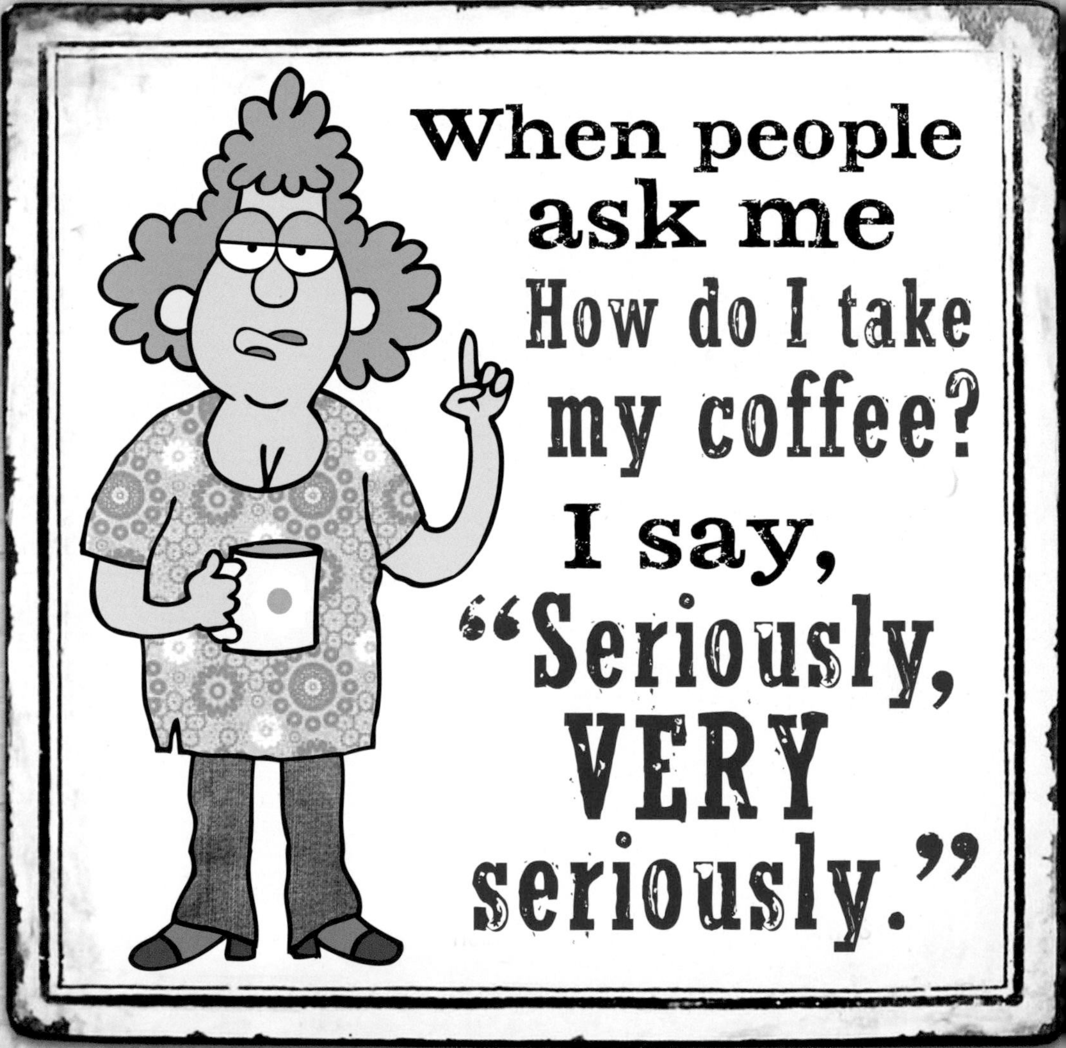
When people
ask me
How do I take
my coffee?
I say,
"Seriously,
VERY
seriously."

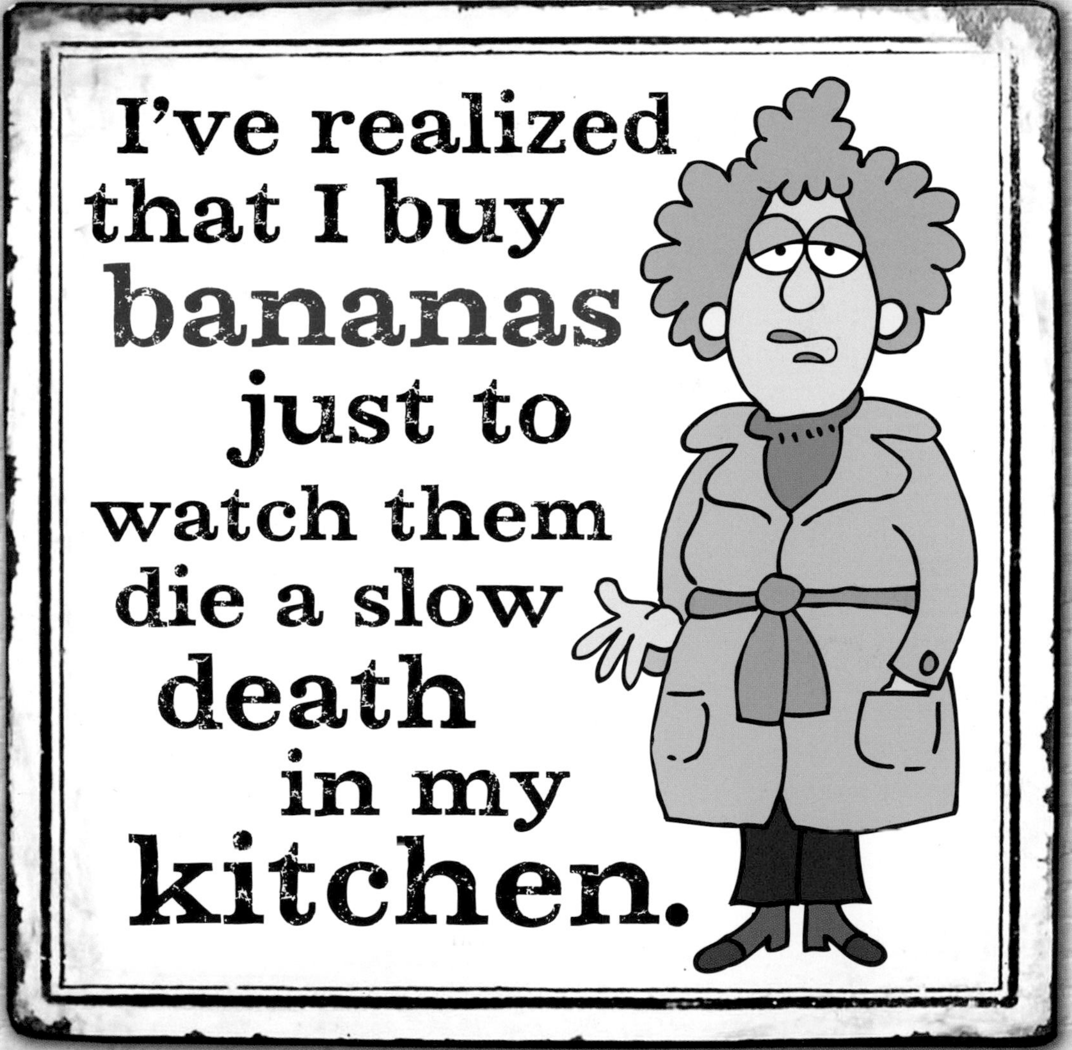
I've realized
that I buy
bananas
just to
watch them
die a slow
death
in my
kitchen.

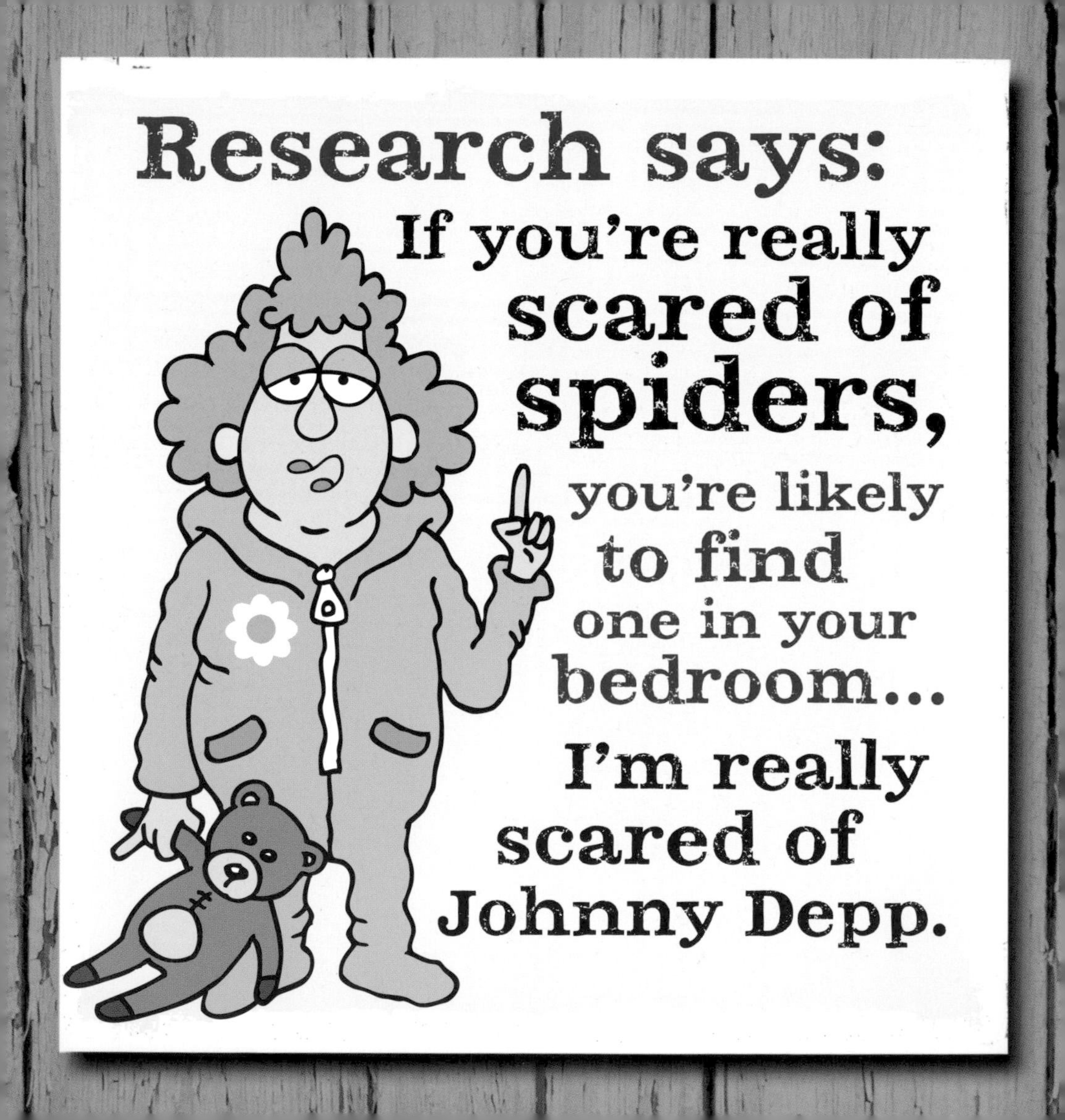
Research says:
If you're really
scared of
spiders,
you're likely
to find
one in your
bedroom...
I'm really
scared of
Johnny Depp.

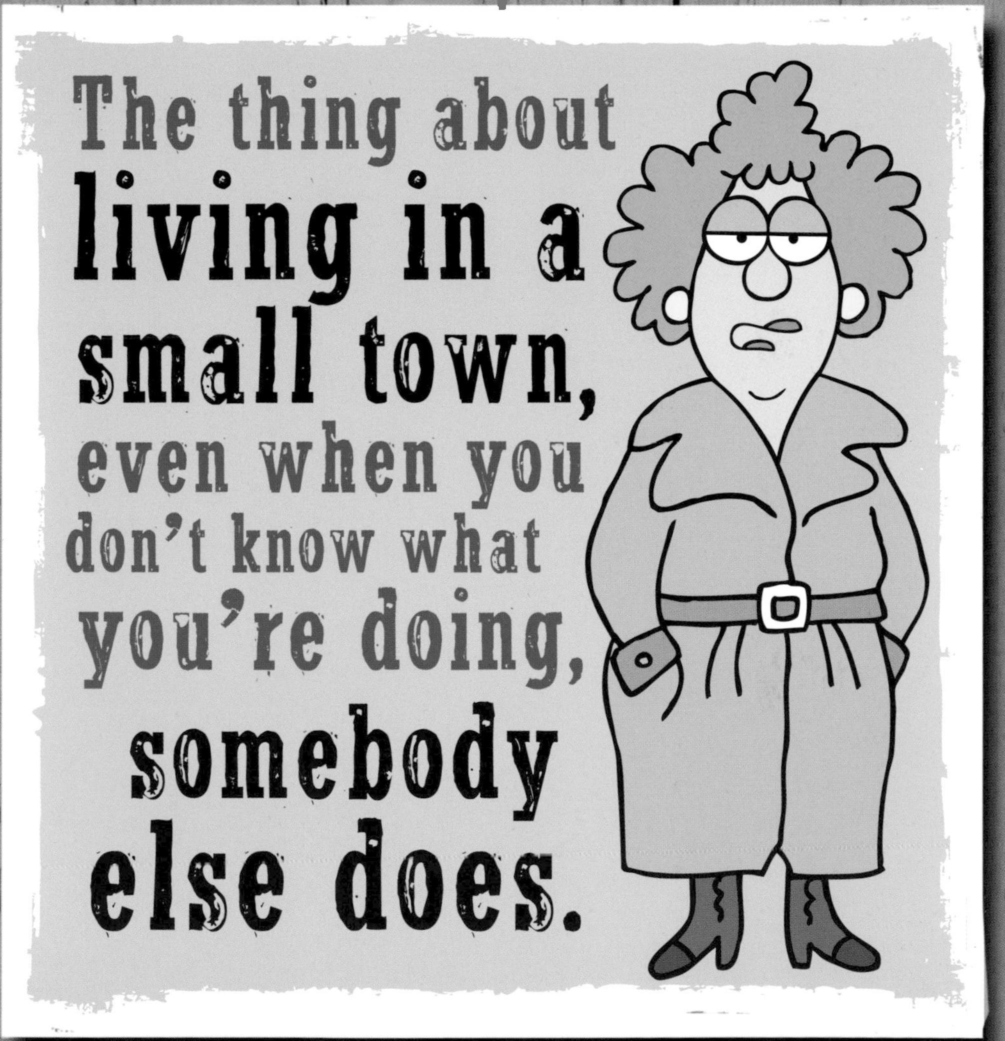
The thing about
living in a
small town,
even when you
don't know what
you're doing,
somebody
else does.

I don't tiptoe through the tulips...

I bulldoze through the bullsh*t.

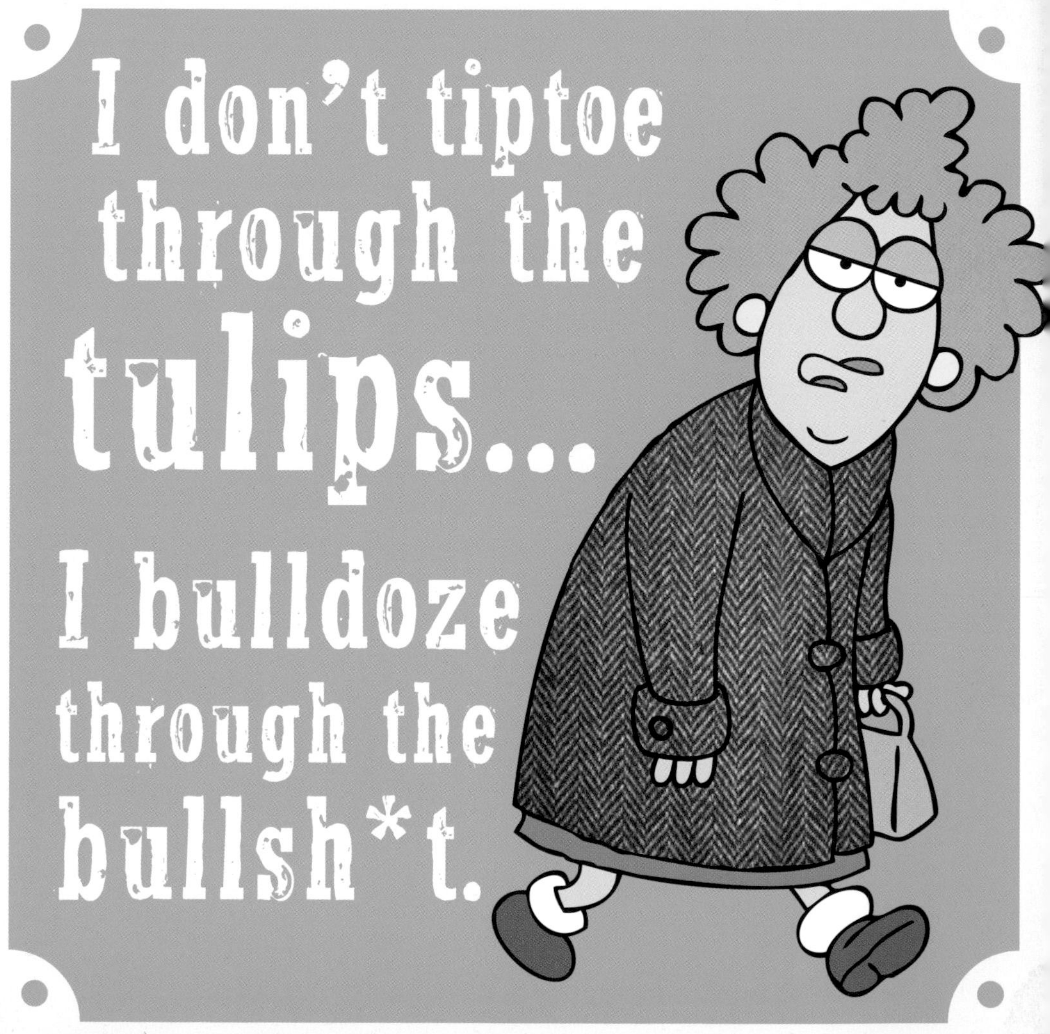

Common sense is like deodorant. The people who need it most, never use it!

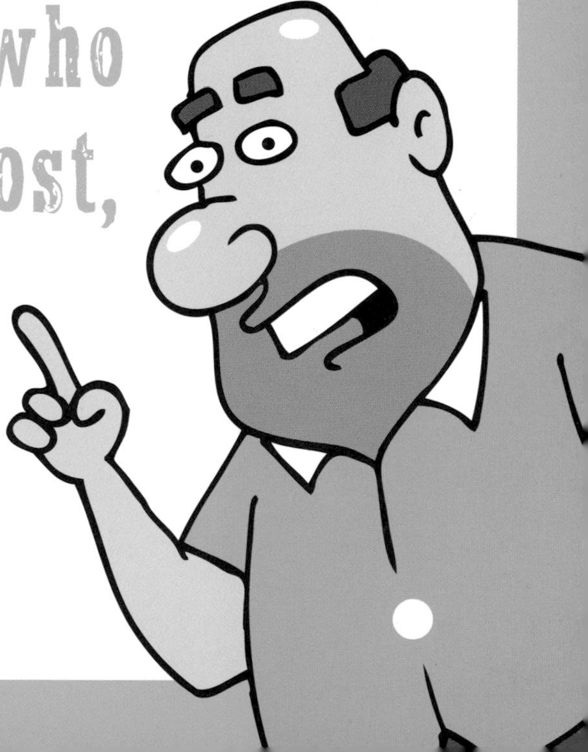

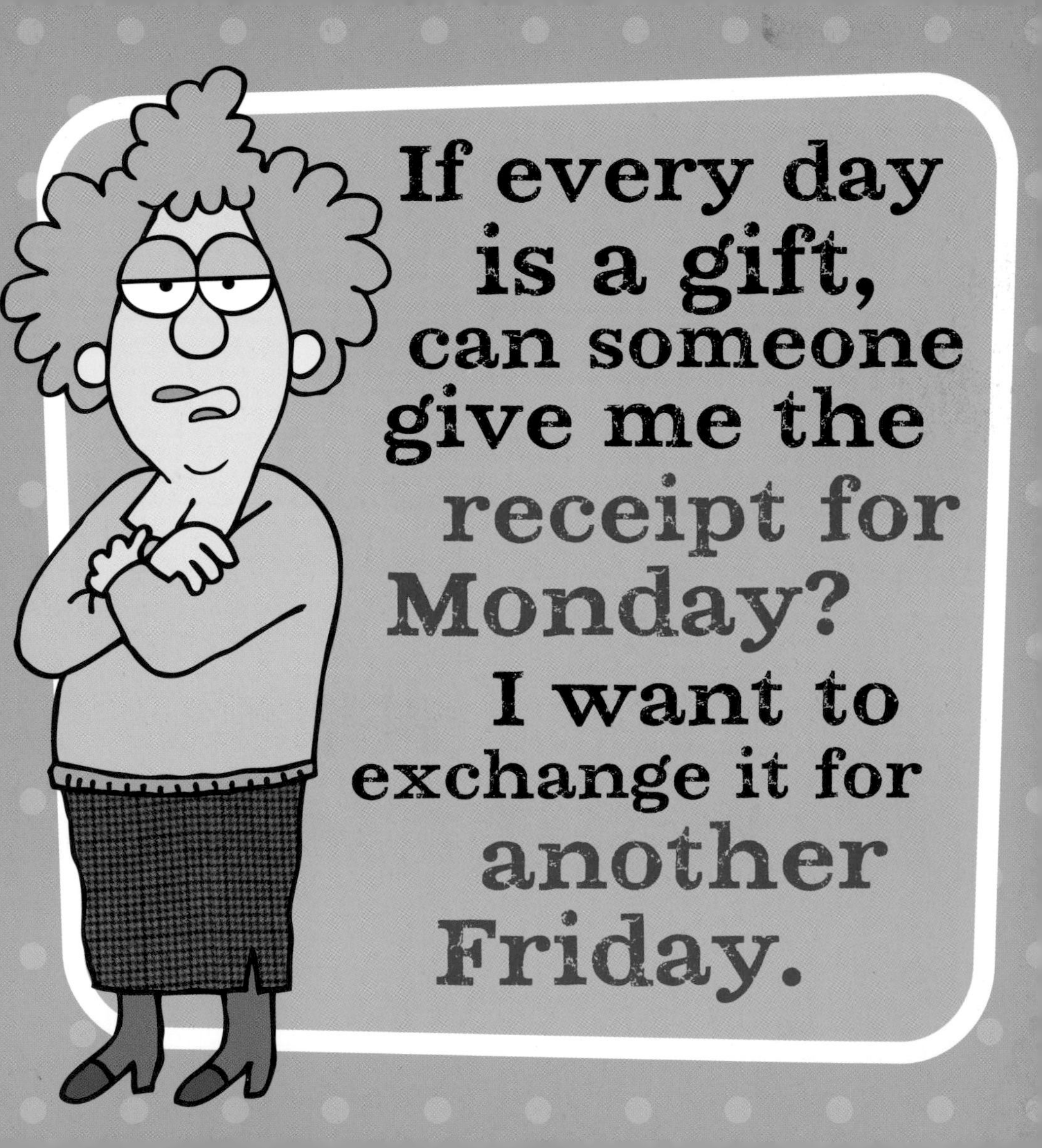

If every day is a gift, can someone give me the receipt for Monday? I want to exchange it for another Friday.

If someone throws a stone at you, throw a flower back at them... just make sure it's still in the plant pot.

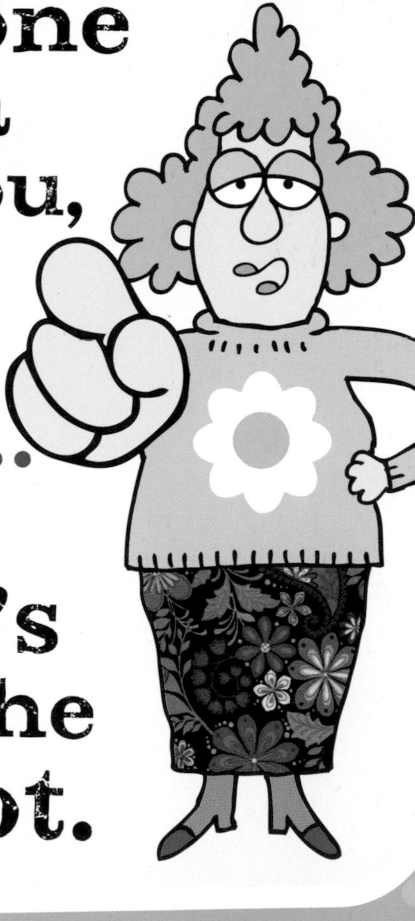

First Edition
18 17 16 15 14   5 4 3

Cartoons © 2014 Ged Backland

Published by
Gibbs Smith
P.O. Box 667
Layton, Utah 84041

1.800.835.4993 orders
www.gibbs-smith.com

Illustrations by
Dave Iddon @
The Backland Studio
Designed by Dave Iddon
Contributed material by
Raychel Backland
Printed and bound in China

Gibbs Smith books are printed
on either recycled, 100% post-
consumer waste, FSC-certified
papers or on paper produced
from sustainable PEFC-certified
forest/controlled wood source.
Learn more at www.pefc.org.

ISBN 13: 978-1-4236-3646-5